KATE TROYER

AN INVITATION TO LET GO OF SHAME
& DISCOVER THE TRUTH OF WHO YOU ARE

SHAME
OFF
you

LIFEWISE BOOKS

shame off you

AN INVITATION TO LET GO OF SHAME
& DISCOVER THE TRUTH OF WHO YOU ARE

By Kate Troyer

Disclaimer: Some names and details were changed to retain anonymity and some characters are fictional yet based on different personality types the author has observed in relationships throughout her life.

Published by:

LIFEWISE BOOKS

PO BOX 1072
Pinehurst, TX 77362
LifeWiseBooks.com

Cover Design and Interior Layout and Design | Yvonne Parks | PearCreative.ca

To contact the author:
KateTroyer.me

ISBN (Print): 978-1-947279-44-5
ISBN (Ebook): 978-1-947279-45-2

dedication

To young Kate:
You couldn't have known what life would look like now, but I think you'd be proud of the person you are today and of the life you created. I'm glad you never stopped dreaming.

special thanks

With gratitude: to my parents, for the difficult choices you made into uncharted waters that provided me the freedom to choose the life I live. Knowing you were raised without affirmation, you still developed the ability to tell me you're proud of me and the life I'm living is an incredible gift. I'm proud of both of you.

Charity Bradshaw and the team at Lifewise Books: Thank you for your dedication and efforts to ensure the words from my heart to paper are presented in a polished form.

table of contents

CHAPTER 1

shame on you

A few years ago, after finding my daughter's room a pigsty yet again, I told her in no uncertain terms, "This is as nasty as a vacated house by one of our tenants!" There—I vented and felt much better. Well, for a minute, until I stopped and replayed what I'd just said. Why did I choose to place shame on my daughter for having a messy room? Why didn't I choose to say, "It really upsets me that you've let your room get so messy. I've told you many times how it bothers me when a room in our home is such a disaster?"

From the earliest age I can remember, I wanted to be loved. My parents did the best they could to express their love to me. It came with simply being held, talked to, and fed. It also came with being yelled at or spanked when I did something I shouldn't have, but most importantly, it came with the emotion that clouded every fiber of my being: shame. It's an emotion that wrestles you to your knees when you'd otherwise brush the lint off your shoulders and purpose to do better. Shame demands that you bow to it, cover yourself in its muck, and punish yourself until you've deemed enough time has passed. With its remnants still clinging to your back like a static-filled sweater, you stand up and limp along.

The culture I grew up in dictated that the ins and outs of everyday life must be orchestrated according to what others think is appropriate. Each act committed was met with, "What would so and so think?"

How many times have you heard the phrase, "Shame on you"? How many times have you bowed your head as its invasive tentacles wrapped themselves around your heart?

I've lived with the constant awareness of other people's opinion regarding the choices I made from a very early age. I was in second grade when my younger preschool aged sister was allowed to go to school with me for the day. The first-grade boy who sat directly behind me began pestering my little sister by tapping her shoulder and whispering things to her. I have no clue what possessed me, but in reply to one of the things he said, I told my sister to say in German, "You still nurse from your mom's nipple!"

He started to laugh. Since it was the noon story hour in our one-room Amish schoolhouse, everyone but the teacher was quietly and intently listening to the next part of the story, when the laugh bubbled over to a full-blown giggle. The teacher stopped reading to ask what was so funny. I froze in my seat! Mortified, red-faced, and afraid of punishment if he answered her question, I was the only person in the classroom not laughing. The teacher asked repeatedly what was so funny. I was ever so grateful that this boy was laughing too hard to answer. He may also have been too embarrassed to tell. I decided I would simply tell the teacher that my sister misunderstood me if I was forced to give account.

Even though I was taught from a young age never to tell a lie, I chose to lie at each embarrassing instance I found myself in to avoid shame. Knowing I'd lied yet again, shame filled me anyway.

At the age of three, as my cousins and I played outside at my aunt's house one warm summer day, I was sitting on the steps outside the kitchen window when I suddenly saw my reflection. Awareness filled my young mind. It was the first time I realized what I looked like. A few seconds later, I heard one of the ladies say, "Look, she's feh spiegel-ing herself!" As they all turned to look, shame filled me as I bowed my head with the realization that it was bad to spend time looking at oneself in the mirror. ("Feh spiegel-ing" = admiring oneself in the mirror.)

Today, I have no doubt that the woman who said it meant no harm and probably thought it was cute, but it was one of the first times I learned that shame was a close companion. Thus, began my aversion to mirrors when others could observe me looking at myself.

Were I not the shy, timid type who internalized everything, I may have grinned widely and ran off to join the other children again. Instead, the bright, sunny day suddenly became dimmer, and I made it my responsibility to do better next time.

At the age of six, I attended the funeral of a young Amish man who hadn't yet joined church. It was doubtful in the minds of those attending whether he was going to heaven, due to his lifestyle choices. Just before the procession to the cemetery began, people began to cry amid the silence. Some wailed loudly. I was so moved with compassion that, despite my best efforts, big, fat tears rolled down my cheeks as I turned to hide my face in my mom's somber, black dress. I felt too ashamed to let others see me cry. Since I didn't know this young man, I thought I shouldn't even be crying.

I frequently questioned why I felt pain so deeply for others. It was too much for my young heart to bear when I couldn't fix things for them. With my personality, it was easy to agree with shame, and it felt like shame was a part of my genetic makeup. I carried it and felt it deeply before I knew the definition of it.

At age seven, as I played with neighborhood children, one of the boys explained to me that his friend could read minds and knew what people were thinking. I was terrified of that boy. I didn't know what reading minds meant, but I wanted to get as far away as possible from him. I was just sure that I would think weird, inappropriate thoughts and feel ashamed because another person would know and judge me for it.

In each experience, fear accompanied the shame I carried. It's little wonder then, that I wilted before others whose personalities were stronger than mine. With each challenging interaction, I buried myself deeper inside the outer shell I had developed. Seeking constantly to go unnoticed, to be invisible and live quietly in my misery, I also desperately wanted to be validated and loved for who I was—not one of many siblings, but one of me.

Growing up one of many children was fun, even if it was chaotic and loud at times. Despite struggling to realize I had a voice, it was the road that brought me to who I am today. Making peace with the bumpy road enabled me to see beauty, where before I could only see pain, shame and loneliness.

CHAPTER 2

not enough

I was conceived in shame. My parents belonged to a church that practiced bed courtship. The couple would spend the night at the girl's house and sleep together for their date, but they were expected not to have sex.

Those who didn't grow up in that environment probably find it impossible to believe that bed courtship could be viewed as a respected way of life. In the church where this practice is upheld, it isn't thought of as strange. It's likely that those who practice it have no knowledge of why it started in the first place; it's just how things are done. This practice is why my parents chose to move to a different community when I reached nine years of age, since they wanted their children to have a different dating experience.

When I was about eight, I overheard a lady saying that a few girls from youth group were being ostracized for choosing to abstain from bed courtship. I heard my mom say it bothered her that a young girl had to take a stand for something most of us would see as a wise choice.

Most young girls from the youth group were able to get away with this practice, but my mom had gotten pregnant. A girl was looked down upon if she got pregnant. Mom was three months pregnant when she married my dad. She carried me, along with her shame, to the day of my birth. I arrived after some complications, and the midwife didn't anticipate a live birth. I began the first year of my life screaming my way into existence. My harried parents tried many things to soothe their new, baby girl, but she wouldn't be comforted.

One evening during revival meetings when I was sixteen, an evangelist heard the confession that I was conceived outside of marriage. He asked my parents to bring me to the meeting early to counsel me and pray over the sin of my life's conception. My heart hurt for the shame I observed my mom carrying for the consequences of her choices. There was a perceived curse on my life because of my parent's sin, and I could tell the evangelist was expecting a powerful confession and redemptive, happy resolution. However, when I was asked how I felt about the way my life began, I simply stated that I was just happy to be here. That was the end of it. The evangelist prayed for me, and I continued with my life.

It is the habit of many professing Christians to put sins in categories. You are in good standing until you commit a public sin. Any girl from the youth group could be having sex secretly and be just fine, but if she got pregnant, she accepted and wore the cloak of shame from then on.

Throughout the ages, women have been judged harshly for having sex outside of marriage, whereas men often get a free pass. The woman is dubbed a whore or harlot. There is no such term for the man.

We women need to know who we are. There may be all kinds of opinions from others, but none of them matter as much as what we know about ourselves. When we don't know who we are, we hustle for our worthiness.

In many religious circles, it's an upheld belief that women are flawed individuals who led the first man on earth astray, and therefore, we must be held subject to men who must decide what is best for us. We are at the mercy of someone else's perception of who we are. Who are we in God's eyes? In Galatians 3:28, the Bible says *"There is neither Jew nor Gentile, neither slave nor free, nor is there male and female, for you are all one in Christ Jesus."*[1] Clearly, it is of the utmost importance that we, as women, know who we are.

Throughout history, the reason women have been seen as second-rate is in part due to their power. Women were given a gift of emotional intelligence and intuition that is different from men. This does not mean men are less than—it simply means women are different. When we find our identity in Jesus and agree with how He sees us, we create a life we're excited to live, not ashamed and not walking timidly, but boldly carving out new paths by the gifts He's given us. It's a lie from man that we are less than and must be held in check. When we're clear about who we are, we will stand up and take our place in our homes, communities, and the world without the yoke of shame.

More harm has been done by men in religious authority who don't have to answer to anyone for their actions and deeds. The situation is largely impacted by women passively standing by, believing they have no authority to challenge wrongful acts. We women often attack each other because we feel helpless in our assigned place. When we see another woman rise up and lead as she finds her identity, we throw daggers her way because surely, it can't be right.

I spent years incredibly frustrated with my place in marriage to my husband of twenty-three years. I waited and waited for him to dream with me and build the life I wanted. I came to the realization that my dreams differ from his. We are two separate people who have different minds and ideas but when flowing in harmony, we bounce our individual ideas off each other and sharpen each other. We dream big dreams and impact the world as a result. My husband has been a solid, strong tower of support. He doesn't always agree, but he wants the best for me, so he lets me breathe and figure out my journey.

All denominations have set beliefs on the place of a woman in the marriage, the home, and the world. Many don't agree with each other. Many denominations don't give room for the context wherein the instructions in the Bible were given. They often embrace the words and seek to apply them literally without examining the history wherein the instructions were given and how they applied to the church at the time. I've found many times when trying to understand the scriptures that I became confused. While many principles of the Bible can be understood and interpreted literally, every denomination differs in their beliefs and is right in their own minds, yet none agree. Many of us spend our whole lives judging each other for wrong beliefs, thinking everyone else is wrong. To me, it's clear to see the importance of receiving the words in the Bible, by the Holy Spirit, so I will understand the mysteries contained therein and they can become life to me.

The church I was born into, taught that if I made a promise before God and man upon being baptized into the church, and I decide to leave, I would go directly to hell. The fear that comes with that teaching is a most effective way to keep people from leaving the church. If we don't learn anything beyond that, we will spend our lives there, hoping to get to heaven by a merit system.

While it's preached we must become born-again Christians, when my parents attended a revival meeting and experienced salvation, they were cast out of the church for a strange belief. We can't know that we're saved, according to the beliefs taught in that church. There are some within each church who believe in experiencing salvation and knowing with assurance that their eternal home is in heaven, but it isn't what the average person from this church believes.

Living in this environment creates the need for law and judgment in each of our choices regarding others, convincing us we must be on different sides. When we have a personal relationship with God, we no longer feel the need to defend our beliefs. Instead, we want others to know Him and experience His infinite love. We entrust them to His care, knowing His DNA runs through their veins just as it does ours (even when they don't know it yet), we no longer feel the need to be their Holy Spirit.

CHAPTER 3

affirmation required

As a teenager growing up in the church, I continually heard of the woman I was intended to become. I sought to grow into a godly woman as instructed, a quiet, meek-spirited woman.

While this sounds good to many, it was a teaching that meant I was to grow into a woman who followed the teachings of the church by agreeing with the men in authority, not questioning anything, and meekly following my husband's leading.

This teaching didn't give room for the verse which says we are neither male nor female in the kingdom of God. These teachings are incredibly effective in driving the belief home that women are not to be trusted because Eve gave Adam the apple in the garden; therefore, women are the ones to be blamed and must be subject to men.

Everything is tainted by this long-held belief. In the church of my youth, the women who attempted to utilize their God-given leadership talents were called Jezebels. It was heartbreaking to watch the attacks these women received from the leaders in the church, and most of them submitted to the attacks and became shadows of the free-spirited girls they once were. Those who couldn't survive left the church. Again, many would still see the woman as wrong, but another person can't teach you how to know God. When we abide by this type of leadership, a woman is required to be content with a relationship with God via her husband.

As a teenager, I was frequently made an example of in the church as the ideal quiet, meek spirited young woman. If anyone could have seen into my heart, they would've seen a desperate, broken girl who had no idea of her identity; thus, she continually submitted to the teachings of the leaders.

The day came when this young woman realized she could no longer survive knowing God only through her dad's understanding and after marriage, her husband. She desperately wanted to know God without the ceiling of a man's perspective. A beautiful thing occurred. One day, the light shone into her heart so brightly that she could never go back to the dark places she had previously inhabited. She knew that God was with her.

Within the church, the women who became dead to their former free-spirited selves were the keepers of the flame. There are few men who notice the small differences in dress; thus, the ways women in this environment supported the men in authority were to point out things that weren't deemed right in the church. The men would then talk to the offender.

When I still believed Eve's shame was my rightful inheritance, it effectively kept me in a place of blind submission. The day I realized that I'm a daughter of the King, I couldn't continue to eat the shame-filled beliefs that I'm second rate.

When we women know who we are in God, and who He is in us, we rise and take our place with authority and walk as He leads. I'm not above my husband. I'm alongside him.

When we seek to live according to the guidelines of man, it causes intense frustration to the grace of God within us. God graced women with intuition, a nurturing heart, and a way of knowing solutions to many issues of the heart that a man is simply not equipped to handle. Men's strengths are manifested differently.

A few years ago, while planning a fundraiser, Sandy wanted to have an idea of how many people to plan for. Her husband said she shouldn't ask people to make reservations because he thought it wasn't necessary. So, she didn't, but she was incredibly frustrated since much of a fundraiser's success comes from effective planning. Sandy didn't challenge her husband's opinion because she believed she needed to be submissive. Instead, she prayed for the grace to forgive her husband. I attempted to hide my disbelief upon hearing her share the story with me. It was difficult for me to understand how even in an area where she had more understanding and expertise than her husband, his opinion could not be challenged.

I remember during the first years of our marriage, asking my husband permission in every situation, regardless how miniscule. A father-daughter relationship proved to be quite unhealthy for both of us. Each time he corrected me or complained about the way I did things, I'd feel devastated. It affected me in the same way it did when my parents corrected me. I felt the need to be reaffirmed constantly—thus each critique caused me to question my value.

It took many years to overcome this way of thinking. Upon recovery, my heart ached for the resentment I held toward my husband, especially since he didn't ask for this position in my life. He was doing his best to wade through all the teachings, too.

Today, I'm incredibly grateful that when my husband occasionally complains about the way I do things, I can simply reply with, "I like the way I do it." We're both okay with it. If he isn't okay a few times, here and there, he'll be fine eventually. There are still times when I forget who I am and revert to being hurt over criticism, but I know I'll be fine again, too.

When I know I'm a daughter of the King, I know I'm enough—not more than my husband, not less than him, but just as much. I'm his helpmeet. We're a team, and when we truly realize we're a team, we're a unit of strength. We're together, us for the world. Our marriage had no way of making it successfully without me realizing my place and identity in God. When God looks at me, He sees Jesus. When I know who He is in me, I agree with Him and see Jesus in me too.

CHAPTER 4

competitive by default

Competition can be a good thing, bringing out the best in us when creating, designing, and playing games. Competition born in shame is another thing altogether, since it hurts those you love and wounds others who are already struggling to find their path through life.

Emelie, a creative, beautiful woman accomplished much in her young life. However, in her eyes, it was never enough. No one else's childhood had been as difficult as hers. Her start in life was bright and filled with promise, but she often ran into trouble because she laughed too loud and played too dangerously. To challenge a dare from a friend was a thrill she was happy to fulfill. Often encouraged to be quiet like her friend, Abby, it frequently pained her heart and left her wishing she could be exactly that.

Meeting with a friend whose personality she admired evoked the need in Emelie to have a grander, more important life to be reassured of her own validity. Emelie's friend Abby lived a quiet, unassuming life. Emelie commented that, "I could never live like Abby, but she is really nice." Each woman who fit Emelie's idea of the perfect person reminded her of her own flaws and insecurities, which in turn evoked the need within her to discredit the other woman.

Emelie became embittered, enraged by the system that dictated what a woman should be, lashing out at anyone who blindly accepted it. Those closest to her suffered much as they sought to appease her anger and remind her that there was beauty in who she was created to be. The challenging journey to realizing that everyone has different personalities with different strengths, and there really isn't a mold, brought amazing freedom to her. Emile eventually realized she was created to lead, to be more vocal than Abby. Once she knew she had the freedom to chase her dreams, and it was a lie to need to feel ashamed for not fitting others' idea of the perfect mold, she began to thrive. The need to be more than her friend dissipated, leaving her able to thrive in her arena. She was able to appreciate the quiet strength Abby lived her life with and chart new roads with her heart wide open.

Candice, a bubbly, compassionate, vivacious woman, brightened each corner of the world she touched, but she carried shame from a disruptive home life with parents who fought loudly and frequently, and life often felt unstable. She coped by glossing over reality and gave room only for rainbows and butterflies. Others talking about difficult challenges frustrated her greatly. She read positive literature and listened to upbeat music, but immediately underneath the surface, rage simmered. When it bubbled over, those in her path scattered, for to be in her line of fire meant to be attacked for how they lived, especially their dysfunctional ways.

While Candice effortlessly saw the dysfunctional ways others lived, she was blind to her own habits of coping, such as disappearing when relationships get difficult or shopping incessantly to make the outside appear better, seeking to cover the void within. Those in her life never knew which version would appear on any given day.

When Candice began to acknowledge the buried pain and allowed God to replace it with His unconditional love, she began to thrive, giving room for bumpy roads and unexpected curves without thinking that her world would fall apart. On difficult days, she took time to breathe, letting the imperfect moments teach her to look at life differently, not demanding that God be as she thought He had to be. Instead, she realized He was always ready to be who she needed in each given moment if she would only ask and listen.

Amie, a strong, reserved, and talented woman, had the ability to accomplish anything she set her mind to. However, she felt she was boring, didn't believe people needed to hear what she had to say, and hid her talent behind busyness. Having long buried the sexual abuse she experienced as a young child, she lived a carefully controlled existence, dressed just so, and shopped for her home relentlessly, constantly seeking to improve on what others deemed perfection.

Amie demanded absolute perfection of herself. She felt strongly about many things, and only occasionally would she express her frustration with a sudden outburst. Regaining control, she lined her ducks up and continued her straight-laced life. After a season of intense illnesses, she began to express her pain in a safe environment, gradually peeling back the layers of long-repressed trauma. She began to realize she did have a voice and that just maybe, others did want to hear her ideas. With a transformation like that of caterpillar turning into butterfly, she began to radiate joy and splash the gift of peace conceived in the darkest moment of her life onto those around her.

As Amie saw herself the way her heavenly Father viewed her, others took notice and found courage to walk through the dark recesses of their own souls, allowing the Father's love to infiltrate each corner, leaving light filled cracks now healed by perfect love.

Kate was a quiet, sweet, and thoughtful woman who loved to serve others, but in her mind, she was as flawed as they come. She had fought anxiety from a young age, thinking often that there was something wrong with her because she couldn't stop the dark thoughts that raced through her mind. Kate used food to fill the pain of sexual molestation that had left its black mark on her soul, but it only resulted in extra weight, which she carried with a heavy cloak of shame.

Kate turned all the rage she felt from the abuse inward, withdrew from the world, and sought to love others by giving of gifts and service. She did these things with a love she couldn't give herself, but alas, she loved with a broken wing. As she spent time seeking the all-elusive God she'd sought after from her youth, she began to see the ways He had been with her all along. She realized that He entrusted her with the dark places because He knew she was strong enough to walk that path. She would bring healing to others as she found peace for turmoil and love for pain.

These examples seek to shed light on the various ways we, as women as well as individuals, see ourselves and cope with our lives. Sadly, some of us struggle most of our lives, hopeless about finding a better, brighter future. We may settle with brokenness, living from a place of bitterness amid the shattered dreams of our youth, presenting a mere shadow of the girls we used to be.

CHAPTER 5

flawed by design

Women are a strong band of warriors, created to be nurturers of the heart and body, with the ability to be soft yet strong, determined yet gentle. When presented with a mountain, they'll scale it, carrying a child in each arm if the need arises. Yet when a woman doesn't know who she is, the impact she'll have on her sisterhood and family can be quite detrimental.

As a young girl, I learned from words spoken by adults in my life that I was flawed. I heard words like "You're not as skinny as your sister, but someone will want you." "You're not perfect, but someone will want you." I blindly believed and accepted that, although I wasn't as desirable a conquest as many other young women, at least a godly young man would want me for my personality. It jived with the deeply ingrained belief that I wasn't worthy of being loved.

As I coped with the effects of sexual molestation from a few different predators and the labels of imperfection, shame piled on top of shame. I developed into a drastically flawed young woman who desired nothing more than to be loved just enough. I expended all my energy to love my younger siblings, do my best to please my parents, and seek desperately to please the God I feared and sought to appease by my efforts. I fell despairingly short.

I loved being a woman, yet I did my best to disconnect myself from my female body. The day I became a woman, with the arrival of my first menstrual cycle, I was devastated. I felt betrayed by my body and thought myself separated irrevocably from a life I could only wish to return to. As I'd done with each life-altering moment before, I wiped my tears, steeled my resolve, and resumed my daily responsibilities.

Hoping against hope, at the age of eighteen I married my husband, anticipating he'd make all my dreams come true. He was to be my knight in shining armor, and we'd live happily-ever-after. I was never more mistaken. The insecurities I brought to our marriage were soon highlighted by the interactions with my new husband. I failed to meet his needs by my inability to successfully keep house and do the things he expected me to fulfill as keeper of the home. Having been accustomed to criticism, I didn't fight back when my husband found faults with me. I accepted it as truth.

I sought to love him with my whole heart, but alas, the struggles in our relationship highlighted my insecurities and left my skills as a wife and keeper of the home wanting. I knew that any holes in our relationship were my fault since my husband was perfect. Believing that my nice personality was the only possible reason he could have chosen me for his partner for life, when he said I was pretty or looked good, I threw it back in his face, refusing to believe his sincerity. I would point out my flaws to my husband, often daily. To the woman reading this, I implore you. Please don't ever point out your presumed flaws to your spouse. Let him think you're beautiful, and let him say it a thousand times if he so chooses.

The defining moments for me—there were more than a few of them—occurred when I began to see that my Father, the king of kings saw me as a beautiful woman, fearfully and wonderfully made. I began to meet the girl in the mirror, whom I'd refused to meet before, with a friendly smile. I began to love her as I loved others. Letting go of the lies I believed and the shame I carried, I accepted the truth that I'm beautiful. I'm worthy of being loved and cherished. I began to love with a love-filled-cracked heart made stronger for having been broken. My children and my husband got more of me; they got my whole heart. I purposed to love unconditionally, as though I'd never been hurt. My tendency before had always been to retreat when someone hurt me.

For the first thirty years of my life, without realizing it, the first thing I did when someone hurt my feelings was to go eat something I thought was unhealthy for me. I drove the pain deep within my heart and added to the brokenness already there. This new love I discovered coaxed me to dare to dream, dare to hope that love wins, love was enough. I expressed my desire to no longer retreat when I was hurt by my husband. I knew I'd often hurt him by hiding within myself, withdrawing my love until I had the courage to stick my neck out again and risk everything to love again. I'm imperfect in this goal, but each time I remind myself that to love is to be vulnerable to hurt. To experience the greatest love, one must allow for the deepest pain.

Raina was born into a chaotic environment. Her father, a quiet, hard-working man, came home each day, exhausted from a long day's work. Quick to give his soft, easy smile to those he loved, he sank deeply into his well-worn easy chair. Her harried mother, exhausted from seeing to the needs of her five young children, would plop the baby on her husband's lap and proceed to lament about all the messes the children had made that day. Father sat, eyes closed, unresponsive to the rambling complaints from his wife. The longer it went on, the angrier Mother got. Her frustration transferred to her husband, and she began to berate him for never listening to her, always working and not helping at home.

With nothing more than a sigh, Father got up, handed the baby to Raina, and went outside. Mother burst into tears. "He never listens to me!" "I have to do everything on my own." Raina held back tears as she hugged the baby to her heart, while Mother continued her tirade against lousy, good-for-nothing men. Raina longed for peace in her home.

Raina's story is yet another example of the effects unspoken thoughts have on us. Clearly, Raina's father was a hard-working man, but he found himself unable to comfort his wife by expressing empathy for her stress. Were he able to express empathy, his wife would have felt validated and found comfort in his recognition of her struggle. While the words Raina's mother spewed at her father were demeaning and hurtful, they came from a place of not feeling heard.

While my way of responding to pain was different than Raina's mother, it was just as harmful. I kept the words to myself, which in some ways was better for my husband, but they ate up my insides, having an impact on my health that left long-lasting effects. It also hurt my husband because I withheld my heart from him, often keeping him guessing as to where he stood with me.

Today, I express my thoughts and feelings much more freely, and while my husband doesn't always like my way of being, he feels confident in my love for him. I don't mind when he doesn't always like my way of being. I'm a work in progress, and I'm okay with that.

CHAPTER 6

practicing gratitude

Gratitude—it's a gift. When we're grateful for the ordinary things, we also notice the little things in life, and our heart breathes a thank you.

My mom read a Bible story to me when I was about seven. It was a story about a boy named Martin who was greedy and always chose the biggest and best of everything. One day, the neighbor lady made fruit tarts for the children. Knowing Martin's tendency, she made one tart bigger than all the rest. As anticipated, Martin quickly scanned the tray of goodies and grabbed the biggest one. Biting into it with gusto, his mouth immediately turned dry as sandpaper, but he choked the bite down. He tried to hide his reaction, since he knew the neighbor lady had intentionally made it for him. He looked around for the trash can. When he thought she wasn't looking, he threw it in the garbage.

That was the last day he ever took the biggest of anything. This had a profound impact on me. From that day on, I was careful to always choose the middle or smaller size of any treat. Those who knew me would know what a challenge that was when it came to baked goods, since I had an intense sweet tooth. Regardless how delicious a brownie looked, I chose to pass up the biggest one.

When I was a little girl, I was afraid of wanting something too much, afraid it would elude my grasp. Early in life, I began to say things such as, "I hope it rains tomorrow," if something like a school field trip or a trip to the zoo was planned. I anticipated not receiving what I wanted. I thought it selfish to voice my preference when presented with first choice for anything, whether it was candy, a toy, or an item that any child would be delighted to receive. I'd do my best to figure out what the other child wanted and choose the opposite. I was much more comfortable letting others choose first.

Today, it saddens me that I was so timid as to think I deserved less than everyone else. I would always take less but feel frustrated with others freely choosing what they preferred, without regard for the person next to them. I secretly envied them.

After I married my husband, I made sure to give him the best piece of everything during the first ten years of marriage. As I began to realize that I'm God's beloved and that He wants to give me good things too, I gave myself permission to choose first sometimes. It took some pep-talks to myself to realize I was not being selfish. I still love giving my husband the best of something, but there are times I choose the best, and it's a wonderful feeling.

"Thou shalt love thy neighbor as thyself…"[1] I found it easy to love others, but it was a long, difficult journey to loving myself. I wore shame and judgment like a well-worn sweater. It was a punishing cloak to wear,

yet I was scared to find out who I'd be without it. What would happen were I to agree with God that when He sees me, He sees His Son? What if I took this verse seriously: *"For I am not ashamed of the gospel of Christ: for it is the power of God unto salvation to everyone that believeth."*[2] Taken from Romans 1:16. What if, in part, this verse means to boldly agree with God and see myself through His eyes?

I don't think God wants to discuss with me the broken identity I had before I knew Him. I think it makes His heart glad when I confidently proclaim who I am in Him—a well-loved, grateful woman who has known dark days and bright days. Regardless of which it is, each morning I choose to say, "It is well with my soul." I love the world as I'm loved and agree with who heaven says I am.

I've encouraged my children to practice gratitude from a young age. When the day was dreary and bad moods abounded, I'd ask for a list of ten things they were grateful for. It took digging deep at times, especially when we'd rather just be mad for a while. One morning, while taking my son to school, I confessed that I was having a very difficult time choosing gratitude that morning. He lit up and quickly said, "Okay, Mom, tell me ten things you're grateful for!" He was delighted to be the one to remind his mom of the thing she preached about all the time. (Insert rolling of the eyes.) There were times I was met with resistance by my children, but by persisting each time, the bad mood was traded for a happy one. It's a wonderful gift to see the things we teach our children sink in.

Over the past few years, our crooked old farmhouse with the uneven floors has been one of my greatest challenges. There have been times when I've stated, "I can't live in this house another year!" The thought that always brings me back to a place of gratitude is reminding myself that there are thousands of people in the world who would feel they'd won the lottery if they suddenly received my house as their new abode—such as the woman who sweeps her dirt floor, ridding it of debris, or the one who places pails around her one-room house to catch the raindrops as they seep through the cracks in the roof.

The truth is, most times when I've been ungrateful for this little, old house, it's because I was comparing what I had to what those around me had. I won't be any happier in a newer, bigger house. It may be nicer, and I'll cherish more space to host family and friends, but if these walls could speak, they'd tell of many funny stories, lots of laughter, important milestones, and sweet memories that have nothing to do with the size of the house.

The timing is perfect for building a new house, and that's what we're about to do. I never imagined it would take fifteen years in this old house to realize our dream, but it was the right amount of time for my heart. When we think we must have more, better, and greater things to be happy, the best gift is to have the more, better, and greater things delayed until we realize it's not in the things we find happiness— it's in choosing to be grateful today, here and now, regardless of the circumstance.

Choosing gratitude means being happy where we are—not waiting for certain people to be removed from our life or having a better job or a better home. We get to choose our attitude; thus, we get to decide if we'll be happy today or not. It's difficult to choose a good attitude sometimes, but life is infinitely better when we learn to be content in whatever state we are in, rather than waiting until everything is perfect to be happy. Life won't ever be perfect. Choose happy!

It's when we're met with people who are difficult to like, challenging jobs, or other such circumstances that we find the important lessons in life that are ours to learn. When we find gratitude in the life we've been given, we won't feel the need to compare our lot with others.

CHAPTER 7

forgiveness

The most painful events in our lives that leave a lasting impact are the avenues whereby we learn the meaning of forgiveness. It doesn't come easy, and there is intense wrestling of the soul on the journey to forgiveness.

From my earliest days, I recall Mom telling me to always look out for others and to never leave a friend outside the circle. My mom had experience with friends excluding her from their circle, leaving a lasting mark on her heart. Despite my desire to honor her instruction, there were times I hurt others by my timid nature, being unable to stand up for what was right.

One afternoon while attending an Amish family member's wedding, I was playing with a few other little girls outside when one of them asked me to play on her family's buggy. We climbed into this unique mode of transportation. As the third girl attempted to climb up after us, the first girl promptly and forcefully informed her she wasn't allowed on her buggy. I felt terrible as the little girl stood next to the buggy, sadness in her eyes, watching us. I wanted to invite her in, but I was intimidated by the first girl and kept my mouth closed.

I've thought of this little girl often over the years, and I can't help but wonder if she remembered this experience as well as I did. While not being the one to exclude her, my inability to stand up to the bully meant my impact was no less. My silence was consent to wrongdoing.

As a little girl in elementary school, a few friends excluded me from their circle for a season. I felt sad but tucked it away safely in my heart. It happened a few more times in adulthood, and I tucked them away as well. Each time, I thought there was something wrong with me and internalized both the experiences and feelings.

When but three years of age, while in the care of others, I was molested by a man. Too young to comprehend what had happened, the shameful experience became a part of my identity.

At the age of five, after an older cousin played doctor with me, an aunt observed it and informed my mom. I was spanked for letting him do that terrible thing to me. I accepted responsibility, decided that I had to be my own protector, and tucked it away in my heart. From that moment, I exhausted myself in my efforts to protect other little girls and was devastated when I discovered I'd been unsuccessful.

From a young age, I began to lie when I felt afraid of punishment. When I did tell the truth and wasn't believed, I decided the truth didn't matter. However, each time I lied, my shame increased.

Throughout my childhood, bad things happened at night, igniting a soul-eating anxiety that peaked after dark. These incidents elicited the response to eat until my stomach hurt, because it would drown out some of the anxious feelings that plagued me. While too much food chased the intense anxiety away for a few moments, it returned in the form of self-loathing for choosing this faulty method of coping.

About the age of twelve, after a series of comments concerning my developing body and its chunkiness, I adapted the belief that I was fat and spent years nourishing that belief. I was quick to inform my friends I was fat before they could think it for themselves. It was most unkind to put the weight of my self-image on my friends. It was more than they should have had to carry, but they were most gracious.

As a young teenager, riding home from church one Sunday afternoon after I responded to something another family member said, my brother turned to me in exasperation and said, "You always say the wrong thing at the wrong time!" Stunned, I gulped and swallowed it. After all, it confirmed my core belief that I didn't have anything to say, or at least, anything worth hearing. I felt awkward and often stumbled over words, and the more stressed I became, the more I stuttered.

At age fifteen, I fell in love with my whole heart. Two years later, that love returned unrequited, leaving my heart shattered in a million pieces. Day by day, I picked up the pieces and continued limping through life, the bag of shame draped over my shoulder growing ever heavier. This taught me the weight of love. It's powerful enough to change a person for the better, or it can break one's heart when the other person's feelings change or aren't reciprocated.

From an age too young to remember, I became the confidant and took on responsibility for the condition of my parent's relationship with each other. Fractured by the things I heard, my relationship with my mom became strained, instilling fear in me to someday have a daughter of my own.

Today, being an adult myself, I understand just how much we all have issues and don't always respond to relationship challenges as we should. Most importantly, I learned the weight a child carries when they're asked to deal with adult issues. The child will eventually despise the parent who hurt the one they love. May grace abound to find forgiveness for each one, as it did for me.

May each adult reading this hear me when I say, it may seem you're winning when you convince your child to be on your side. Trust me when I say, it's only short term. I don't think it's the parent's intention to harm the child's relationship with their other parent. The person is in a lot of pain and wants to be understood, but the child, while lending an ear, is incapable of handling the adult issues. A child will experience lasting harm when asked to choose one parent over the other. Long term, it doesn't work.

Throughout my teen years, after hearing repeatedly in the church about all the things potentially hidden in one's heart, I confessed to a wide variety of sins that I didn't commit. I was desperate to be free of shame, ever digging through the layers of my heart, attempting to uproot any possible, hidden sin—yet still, peace eluded me.

All these things, along with the shame my parents and their parents before them carried, summed up my identity. But were all those things really me? Is that who I am? Is that all I am? How would I overcome all the things I was taught that had contributed to my emotional and physical state of ill health? The following verses brought light to the darkness I'd been immersed in, and I found the truth of who I am lies in this:

> "*I am fearfully and wonderfully made: marvelous are thy works; and that my soul knoweth well.*"[1]

"The Lord hath appeared of old unto me, saying, Yea, I have loved thee with an everlasting love: therefore, with lovingkindness have I drawn thee."[2]

"Before I formed thee in the belly I knew thee; and before thou camest forth out of the womb I sanctified thee, and I ordained thee a prophet unto the nations."[3]

Upon realization of this truth, the events that shaped my reality and defined me were gradually replaced with the truth of who God says I am—revelation by revelation. Much of the junk I held onto kept me from clearly seeing my true identity. But as my mind continues to be renewed, I also continue to identify more with God's view of me.

Before this, I found it impossible to overcome the forces that shaped and defined me, uncomfortable living without the identity of a flawed, molested, self-harming girl. After learning who God thinks I am and embracing my identity in Him, I found the grace to forgive all. Unforgiveness was not allowed to continue taking up space inside my heart. It had to go, for life and death couldn't abide together within me. I wanted to live more than I wanted to keep the identity I'd been comfortable with, though I was broken.

CHAPTER 8

mistaken identity

How many times have you heard, "Look at what she's wearing!" or "I wouldn't be caught dead wearing that!" and many other such comments? Women can be incredibly cruel to each other.

The other day, while out on a lunch date with my husband, I overheard two ladies at the table next to us discussing one of their friends. If the friend would have heard those unkind comments, she would have questioned whether she was truly their friend. I remarked to my husband that the conversation I heard was typical of other times I've overheard ladies gossiping.

As a pre-teen, I overheard an adult in my family say that a certain young woman from the church youth group thought she was quite something. A few weeks later, another young lady from youth group stated that her friend was incredibly beautiful. I repeated what I'd overheard. The stricken look the friend responded with had a lasting impact on me. I realized I said something unkind and purposed never to utter such a comment again. It was a dramatic teaching moment in my young life. Over the years, I have pondered why the adult in my life felt compelled to make that degrading remark.

Unfortunately, this was not an isolated incident. Why do women often treat each other so harshly?

Do we not realize we're sisters, and we are each other's keeper? We rant and rave about women's rights and rage against men for deeming us second rate creatures, but who really is doing the accusing? Who said we're second rate, and why did we believe it?

What stands out to me from my childhood in the Amish church was the many times I heard comments from the older women in the district. "I feel sorry for that little girl. Her parents gave her such a worldly name." Or, "Did you notice that young woman wears her 'kapp' too far back on her head?" (A kapp is a head covering worn by Amish women.)

Many times, the women would be friendly to a person's face, but turn around and make derogatory comments to another sister in the church whom they felt would agree with them. Many times, since gossip travels as it does, the comments are carried back to the victim of the gossip.

Why do we gossip? Is it not due to secretly knowing we are living a dried-up life, void of passion and excitement for what we anticipate accomplishing next? Since it's dictated that we must live within the confines of what all the others deem acceptable, we lash out at those who have the courage to buck the system and do what they desire.

In my experience over the years, I've found myself in many situations where mean comments were made about a mutual friend. I regret to admit, I've been lax far too often in responding as I should have. If I'm silent or laugh when something mean is said about an acquaintance, I'm just as guilty as the one who uttered the words.

It's far from popular to speak up and tell another person what they just said isn't right. Often, it's met with a comment such as, "There's something wrong with Kate," "She was really defensive of our friend," or "I wasn't being mean, I was just stating the facts."

I truly realized the impact of such comments when they were relayed to me. Statements such as, "I could never live like Kate does, but at least she's nice," or, "I feel bad for Kate, she must feel so uncomfortable with how she looks," or "Kate is really nice, but she's very standoffish, and she has some serious issues."

I've been guilty of unkind comments about another. I justified my comments because I thought my friend was wrong for the choices they made. Why, then, did I feel empty and the pit of my stomach filled with dread? Experiencing some of the comments made about me and the pain it accompanied taught me the weight of a careless comment I've made about another woman—especially if that woman heard what I had said. Why do I think it my business to comment on someone else's choices, just because they're different than mine?

Why are we happier to cut our sisters than to lift them up and allow for their journey to self-acceptance and embracing the one who's fearfully and wonderfully made? It breaks my heart, realizing the impact it has when we cut each other—and ultimately, when cutting each other, we cut ourselves. We are, out of many, one.

Do we secretly think if we compliment others, it means we're not as good as they are? Do we believe we must cut others to ensure we're enough?

I imagine we will be amazed at the transformation in womanhood when we begin to embrace each other, flaws and all, supporting our sisters in their respective journeys through life. Our strength is in remembering we're on the same team. We divide while seeking to conquer when we spend our time talking negatively about each other.

We may, at times, reduce ourselves to competing for a man's attention, or fight another woman for her position, failing to realize, we're worth entirely too much to compete like this. Our individual, unique perspective means there's room for each of us to live our lives without needing to win a competition to prove our worth.

May each of us decide to live true to the convictions of our heart; may we chase our dreams and be so busy living our life and rowing our own boat, we won't have time to comment on how someone else rows theirs. May we be so secure in our identity that we freely compliment others and call out their true identity. We can know their journey doesn't compete with our own, for each one of us is unique, and no other's story is the same as ours.

CHAPTER 9

evil surmising

A few years ago, I experienced a difficult period with some of my family members. At a holiday get-together, a disagreement erupted between a few of my sisters due to a struggle they were working through. As usual, with a large family, such eruptions splash on and affect others. In trying to listen to each of my sibling's perspectives, there was an incredible amount of turmoil as I waded through all the emotions hurtling at me from different directions.

Ever the peacemaker, this wasn't the first time my attempts to fix things backfired. One sister saw the situation a specific way and the other sister saw it from her unique perspective. I was swayed as I tried to hear each one and give objective feedback yet not feed the pain that each one's specific view caused them.

What transpired over the next twenty-four hours left me reeling as I tried to pick my own heart up off the floor again. In revisiting the debate that transpired, I realized that my passionate response to protect one also hurt the feelings of the other. My support of the one was interpreted as not supporting the other. I understood the pain each one felt, but they were not ready for a solution. Their emotions ran too high. It was a time for waiting and reflecting.

As I sought to make peace with the effects of the storm, I wanted to nurse my own pain. I was hurt, and I had the right to be hurt. I felt a variety of emotions while seeking peace with the situation. In the conversations that transpired, accusations towards me from earlier occasions were shared with me that I hadn't been privy to. This intensified the pain and mistrust I felt toward my sisters.

I realized quickly that I had a choice. I could let all the things I heard convince me I didn't have the support of my sisters, or I could look at their hearts and choose to focus on the love each one sought to live by. When I made the conscious decision to not embrace the painful accusations, peace flooded my soul. Each time the painful thoughts sought to return to invade my space, I responded with, "I choose to focus on their intentions, and I know their intentions toward me are good."

Were each of my sisters to write their life story, you probably wouldn't realize we're from the same family. We each see life through our own set of glasses and view life according to our experience. Being aware of this fact helped me to return love for anger, peace for pain. Each situation we face allows us to either feed pain and suspicions about others, or feed love and acceptance. I seek to feed love and acceptance.

The verse that came to life for me during that time was; *"He is proud, knowing nothing, but doting about questions, and strifes of words, whereof cometh envy, strife, railings, evil surmisings."*[1] It challenged me to be aware that I'm not a mind reader. I may think I know what someone else is thinking, but many times I have been wrong. When through the eyes of pain, I imagine what others' feel about me, many times, I'll get it wrong.

We learn to love according to our comprehension of it. Many times, we love imperfectly since we're still carrying the shame, guilt, and pain of unfinished emotional turmoil from previous trauma.

Have you noticed that there are people in your life who clearly lie about how things really are? What if it's their perspective, and thus, to them it is true? What if the pain of the emotions they carry makes it impossible for them to embrace reality and allow the pain of what was, to be turned into peace? We often demand others see life as we do, which is often the reason why there's so much heated discourse among us.

We often demand the most from those closest to us. We give grace to friends for their imperfections but frequently criticize those we love most. Often, our response doesn't feel much like love at all, but when we love them even in their imperfections, we'll find it enables them to receive God's love more freely.

Most times during painful interactions with those we love, we accept the lie that the other party's intention was to hurt us, that they have it in for us. What if we start asking, "How can I understand this person better and understand their point of view?" or "How can I show love and acceptance?"

People ask for love in the most unlovable ways when they need it most. My habit, for much of my life, has been to withdraw when someone asks for love in a difficult way. What if I allow vulnerability to the point I give the unlovable acting person room to be as they are, until they receive grace to ask differently? What if I choose to love anyway?

Expecting someone else to accurately sense what we need is often a setup for disappointment. Many times throughout our marriage, when I felt unloved, it was because I anticipated my husband would realize he should help me when I was stressed. Instead, he didn't notice, and I took personal offense. I added the offense to all the others piled up on the shelves of my heart and continued on this dysfunctional path for many years. Today, I realize that when I need help, I need to ask for it; thus, my husband doesn't need to guess what I want or wonder why I seem withdrawn.

Even when you've been hurt by others' actions and words thousands of times, see the best in them anyway. Look behind the actions and words of the hurting person and remind them of the truth of who they really are: a beloved child of the King of Kings, whose DNA runs through their veins, the lover of our souls, the redeemer of our dark places, and the mender of our broken hearts.

CHAPTER 10

she's perfect, i'm not

When we're ashamed of who we are, we hide from others. We try to appear as we think the other person is. When we fail to live authentically, we're constantly concerned about how others view us. We may be hard on our family members because they frequently embarrass us. We would give anyone else's family member the room they need to be who they are. If they do something embarrassing, we find it humorous and endearing. When it's our family, we cringe and complain about their inappropriate actions.

Being authentic means to be you, not someone else. When you try to fit in with others, the world doesn't get to experience who you are and what you'd contribute with your individual and unique talents.

The best gift we can give our children in this world is to encourage them to be their own special flavor. There will always be children who will say hurtful things and lack the ability to be empathetic.

Some parents believe in letting their children do as they wish and let them sort out the pecking order by themselves. While figuring out the pecking order is a good idea in part, by discouraging helicopter parenting, some children only learn empathy by parental input.

At times, much to the frustration of my children, I fell somewhere in between helicopter parenting and letting them figure things out for themselves. I did ask that they show kindness toward others. Many times, my son would be incredibly upset with me. He'd remind me repeatedly how he's the only one who must be kind, other kids don't have to. As much as he didn't appreciate my feedback at the time, I'd explain to him that the only person we can control is ourselves. It takes more strength to be kind than to hurl words that wound the heart.

When we encourage our children to be themselves despite negative comments from others, we give them a platform to touch the world. Trying to fit in is what makes a student popular in school. They find a few others like themselves, leaving the rest of the students with low self-esteem seeking to fit in or suffering greatly when they can't fit in.

The desire to fit in is dramatically noticeable in the adult world also. It's probably the primary reason so many children suffer from bullying. Bullying has been around for ages. It's an ugly thing, but how much more impact would we have if we inspired our children to be themselves? Too often, we help them fit in with all the right clothes and secretly feeling proud if they happen to fit in with the popular children. How much more positive would our impact be on those around us were we to choose authenticity instead of fitting in?

The culture I grew up in was dramatically influenced by what everyone else thought about each other. We had to do everything according to set standards from the church. When someone chose to do differently, she was immediately in the line of fire from other women in the church. Much of what is deemed acceptable is dictated by the women. Most men don't notice little differences in dress code.

One simple example is that the church community we moved to when I was nine years old required braiding the girls' hair until they were teenagers and could do their own hair. Having come from a community where girls didn't wear braids, my mom kept doing our hair the way she'd always done it. This was discussed by the women who'd always braided their daughter's hair. They frowned upon this new way of hair styling. Yet, after a season, others began to do hair as my mom did. Soon most women stopped braiding their daughters' hair.

It seems when we're raised in religion, we're predisposed to want rules to live by to feel safe. For example, in the many different religions and denominations within Christianity, each church judges the other and believes their beliefs are right and others are wrong. This plays directly into the drive to conform to everyone else.

When some fail to conform, they run into trouble with the church. We tend to make the things we believe of greater importance than the condition of the heart. We so often judge others on the outward appearance. When someone does all the right things, we embrace them as wonderful, godly people. However, when someone does something we deem wrong, we rush to judgment and pick up our rocks, ready to begin throwing stones to make sure others know we're separating ourselves from the sinner.

When we judge others by their outward appearance and overlook what often hides in the heart, it makes it easy for sexual abuse, physical abuse, and other harmful behaviors to run rampant, since the things done behind closed doors go unnoticed. When we live by the approval of others, we compromise our own conscience, and we continue living in our dysfunction.

Many times within the church, victims of abuse continue to exist without a voice because of the power of shame that accompanies abuse. Many times, the victim becomes ostracized and is accused of lying. Having had first-hand experience with sexual abuse, I know the shame it held over my head, the silence it demanded of me, and the accusations I felt.

When we're afraid to be genuine, we are quick to draw attention to the offender, lest others think we're friends with the wrongdoer. We judge lest others see into the recesses of our own heart and realize we make wrong choices also.

Many times, when something happens to a woman, the first response from other women is, "She was asking for it." or "What does she expect, being dressed like that?" Again, I ask, who is doing the oppressing? Where are the ones who rush to the woman's side to support her and hold her hand? Do we not often judge her first and discuss her with our friends?

Could it be that women are the reason we believe we're less than men? The cruelty and competition among women toward each other can be staggering. Have we forgotten that we're sisters? Have we forgotten that men will scale mountains and slay dragons to win a woman's heart? Are we trying so hard to be everything a man is, to prove ourselves equals, that we forget men and women are completely different and therein lies our strength? Women are everything men aren't, and men are everything women aren't. That's our gift.

We'll accomplish a lot more when we support each other instead of competing with each other.

CHAPTER 11

lack of education

The lack of formal education has harmed many women's self-esteem by instilling the belief that, since they don't have as much education as others, they're less than. Some of the most brilliant people I've read about had a parent with little education, but they had a love of learning. They instilled in their children the importance of practicing gratitude and kindness.

A formal education, while a great gift, isn't required to live by the most important mottos in life. There was a time when we didn't have access to all the information we do today, and education was harder to come by. Today, we get to learn by studying with books from the library or classes online. The important thing is to be hungry—hungry to learn, love, and grow.

In today's world, many times a well-qualified person will be passed over due to a lack of college education, and the one who went to college gets hired for the job. Decisions are often made by looking at a paper as opposed to using some of the skills utilized from days gone by. For example, my husband and I have been stewards to the best of our ability, paid our bills on time, and developed a good credit record. However, when it came time to borrow money for further investing, we ran into a problem. A number of banks only looked at the paper; it didn't matter to the bank that we had proven good stewards of the money we borrowed, because they only made their decision based on what the paper showed. Back in the day, if you had good credit, paid your bills on time, and had collateral, a banker would be happy to further invest in you.

My point is simply to show that in today's world, many things are backwards. Words on paper mean more than the character of a person. I understand that many banks have been left hanging with mortgages people dropped when the housing market fell, in large part to banks' lending more than a property was worth. Some people saw the chance for a "get-out-of-jail-free card" and took it. Banks took a big hit, but it also harmed those who did right by the banks. This is, of course, just one aspect of things.

I went to a parochial school through eighth grade, and to many people, that means I'm uneducated. The truth is, I educate myself. In the area of functional medicine alone, I've dedicated more than twenty years to learning everything I possibly can about the body and its functions. In doing research, I've realized that our way of doing life today, health wise, is quite different than it used to be. We used to use food to nourish our body. Today, you're considered a crunchy Mama if you use natural ingredients for health, as opposed to relying on your doctor for your health. Because of what I've researched, I have confidence and don't live in fear of sickness and disease. I don't look to my doctor for health advice; I rely on him for an emergency, but I use what I've learned to make healthy decisions for my family and myself.

I read almost every day. Reading is one of the best gifts we've been given. I'm ever so grateful to have been gifted with the freedom to get an education. While according to the educational standards of today, I may be less educated, there are still many places in the world where education is a luxury, and many women would be excited to have the opportunities I have.

Regarding education, the best gift teachers and parents can give their children is to teach them not how to think but learn to think for themselves. Many mothers of famous people today, who were themselves uneducated, instilled in their children the belief that they could accomplish anything they set their minds to.

How many times over the years have you heard an adult say to a child, "You need to choose a realistic career?" Or if the child chose a difficult career, the parent helped guide them to something less challenging.

A few years ago, my daughter, in response to my comment that she was naturally gifted with a good singing voice, replied with, "Mom, I had an interest in singing, but I wouldn't be good if I didn't practice developing my voice." This was a teaching moment for me. I thought back over my youth and realized that as a young girl, I had an interest in cooking. My mom turned me loose in the kitchen to learn. Had I not practiced, I wouldn't have become a good cook. Practicing and watching from other cooks increased my skill level.

I spent many years waiting for God to reveal what my calling is and show me the path I should choose. I resented my husband because I was taught that I must let him make the decisions, and I had to make my dreams fit his. When I realized he wasn't my ceiling, and he didn't want the position of making all the decisions for us, I began to take my place alongside him and we chose together. When I had an interest that he didn't, I did something on my own, and it was the same for him. It has proven healthy for both of us to have some independent interests. Could it be that instead of waiting for God to drop the right path in front of us, He gifted us with interests? When we feed that interest, we become good at it and therein find our career path?

The quote, "A ship's sails can't be adjusted while still in the harbor" has had a major impact on me. For many years, I thought I was supposed to wait on God to show me my life path. Upon hearing this, my eyes opened to see that God had created me with gifts, interests, and talents to nurture; thus, if I nurtured them, I would become good at them. The best caterer didn't become one except by practicing. The best gardener didn't get a green thumb but by practicing gardening. The gardener had a seed of interest, planted it, and through trial and error, became one of the best. The sails of a ship can always be adjusted on the journey.

We have the freedom to become anything we want. When we belong to a church that doesn't allow certain things, then we have a choice to make—the choice to conform or break the mold. The choice is still ours.

Men in certain cultures dictate what woman may or may not do concerning education. When did that become so? If Eve was wholly responsible for the fall of man, thus women need to be kept subservient, doesn't that suggest that women by their God-created beings are powerful? How many stories have you read in which men did crazy things to win the heart of a woman? Does this not suggest that the belief that women are less than men, is a lie? Could it be if we as women were to realize this and lead our lives with the authority

God gave us, the men would happily find balance and begin to slay dragons and scale mountains to win our hearts, happily protecting and serving their woman?

The fact that we rail against men and believe we must push them down for us to have the same freedom suggests that maybe the problem lies in us not knowing who we are. When men do crazy things to win a woman's heart, it means he knows she's a powerful being and wants to prove himself worthy of her. Why do we at times compete with another woman to win the affections of a man—a woman who knows her worth, won't engage in fighting for a man, because she knows she's worthy of a good man.

Today, more than ever, we have a whole world of opportunity before us. When we put our hearts into it, we're unstoppable. This doesn't mean everything comes without a fight. Sometimes there's intense opposition from those close to us, but when we know who we are, and lead from a place of confidence in our identity, others will eventually have to take their hands off and allow the woman to lead as God called her.

CHAPTER 12

tell your story

Before I wrote my first book, I had this bizarre fear that were I to share my experience with someone else, they'd steal my story. Maybe that fear had something to do with coming from a large family where one can get lost in the quantity of people and individuality can be hidden, but when I gave voice to this fear, I realized how silly it was.

Each of us has a story to tell, a life to live. I believe the fear I had was the result of not knowing myself. I was created as an individual, and therefore, no one can steal my voice. It was a lie to believe that someone else could read my heart to the extent they could steal what was mine.

When we know who we are, we know that we have our own life—one voice and a unique perspective to tell our experience. Without knowing this, we compete and at times seek to harm each other's reputation out of desperation to be validated.

Sally was a lovely, talented young woman who had many friends but continually saw herself as not enough. She believed everyone else had life better and easier than she did. Looking from the outside in, Sally appeared to have it all. She had a wonderful career, a beautiful family, and a good husband. Her belief that she was less than others created a negative reaction toward other women. When someone complimented one of her friends, she'd add a cutting remark to lessen the effect of the compliment on her self-esteem.

It was unclear whether Sally realized she had this habit, but it seemed involuntary. She couldn't figure out why she struggled to have close friends. When she began to see that she was a daughter with a unique voice and felt loved by her heavenly Father, she began to sow loving words instead of cutting comments. Suddenly, women were drawn to her and began to seek out her company, not knowing what they sought, just knowing they loved how they felt when with Sally. She was amazed by the transformation of her life.

How often do we spend time mulling over the fact that our life is uneventful and unimportant? It may not be nearly as glamorous as the friend next to us. We see what is presented to us, what another allows us to see. It may look perfect from the outside, but within each person's life are struggles to overcome, habits to change, and ways of being that inhibit our best life. When we are allowed a glimpse into the person's life, we come away surprised that all isn't perfect.

At times, while feeling unsatisfied with our own life, we lash out at others by commenting on something they do that we would never do. We shamefully feel a little better when things don't go well for them in a certain area. When we know whose we are and who He is in us, we choose to bless and encourage others, and when things go unwell for another, we reach out to them and support them in their struggle.

Many times, we feel angry toward others for acting and living imperfectly and seek to correct those we love. Loving them by giving them room to be who they are and reminding them of their identity brings them to the awareness that they're whole, complete, and wholly loved.

The Father's heart is good toward His children. He provided a way for us to live bountifully, joyfully, and contentedly, regardless of our current situation. When we know His heart, we don't fear our future. Many times, our biggest challenge is overcoming the hurdles of teachings we heard or were taught while we were growing up. It's my experience that most of the teachings I grew up with, led me further from God's heart, since they made me afraid to trust my heart to Him. I lived in such fear of His wrath that I was afraid to have honest conversations with Him. I wouldn't have dared express anger with Him.

Many times, I've been angry with Him, voiced my frustrations, and in the middle of my tirade, I suddenly saw a new truth. My heart melted as I imagined His grin over all my blustering. There've been many times when I sheepishly apologized for my self-righteous outburst. His grace is the most amazing gift, encompassing everything He is. Each time, I realize a new truth and, once again, I'm amazed by who He is. I discover a new piece of His heart and fall deeper in love with Him.

When we know God only by the teachings of others, we are kept at their mercy. When we have a personal relationship, our interactions with Him always remind us of how heaven sees us. When we agree with His view, we become confident of our identity in Him. We walk on this earth with authority and compassion, loving others to Him.

Religion often dictates that others clean up their act before we accept them, instead of allowing Jesus to win each person by His gentle drawing of their heart. We often separate ourselves from those deemed unrighteous, lest we be thought of as the same. Jesus was called a winebibber by those who had a problem with his friends. Could it be that He didn't go to church regularly like the others? Could it be that He spent more time in the highways and byways, winning hearts by love rather than judgment?

Growing up, I was taught that we're to be the salt of the earth; however, when someone appeared ungodly, I believed I had to separate myself from them. The One within me wasn't deemed strong enough to influence good over bad.

When we know we're born of Him, everything points to Him. We portray His love and reveal His heart by His habitation within us. Our life bears the fruit of His goodness. We show compassion where religion demands judgment. We choose to look like a fool rather than throwing someone to the wolves.

When we know our identity, we unapologetically tell our story. We no longer fear what others think of us, because we're secure in the Father's love for us and confident in His acceptance.

CHAPTER 13

less opinions, more listening

A few weeks ago, my daughter, suffering terribly with eczema, was at her wits end. She had started working at the community hospital a few months before. When I asked if she was required to get the flu vaccine, she told me she didn't. I was surprised because I had heard that everyone who works at hospitals was obligated to get the vaccine or be terminated. After she tried many different things for her eczema and feeling hopeless, I asked her again if she'd had the vaccine. I quickly explained that I wouldn't get mad if she did, I just wanted to help. She admitted that she did get the vaccine. She'd never had a hint of eczema before. It made sense, based on my personal research, that the chemicals in the vaccine could have caused her skin's reaction.

Because people close to me had had a dramatic reaction to vaccines, I was quite outspoken and passionate about my stance on them. I was on a health mission and defensive when others were called terrible parents if they didn't allow vaccinations. I frequently spoke to my family about the things I learned from my research. The problem with my mission was that my passionate opinions made my daughter scared to admit she had taken the vaccine. This caused her a lot more pain than if she had been able to talk to me about it.

We were able to find a natural solution, and her skin dramatically improved in a very short amount of time. Had I listened more than given my opinion, my daughter would've felt comfortable to tell me she was required to get the vaccine. After she told me about it, I explained to her that if she decided to get it again, there were natural things we could give her before and after, to lessen the impact it had on her body.

A few years ago, a friend of mine had decided to work full-time soon after her daughter was born, while her husband worked less time. Thus, he was often the baby's caretaker. I was quite opinionated that a Mom's primary responsibility was taking care of her baby. I commented one day that a child needs their mother, and how it's not good for the mom to leave the new baby for long hours every day. The dad overheard my thoughts. I have no doubt I either offended him or caused him pain because I was clearly stating that my friend was erroneous in her decision to work full-time.

May I just ask, "Who made me boss?" Reflecting on experiences like these has humbled me to my core. It is one thing to be passionate about something, but when I am passionate about something to the point of believing I have the right to decide what's best for someone else, it's simply arrogant.

I no doubt alienated that friend because of my words. There are so many areas in life in which we all have different beliefs and ideas about what's best. It's okay to be different. Each mom loves her child to the best of her ability. That's what counts. Even when we try to be the perfect mom, we fail. That's okay, but when we realize we've made mistakes, if we humble ourselves, we become more compassionate.

I chose to live in a little old house so I could be the primary caretaker of our children, rather than have a career so we could afford a bigger, better house. That was my choice, and I wouldn't have traded it for the world, but it's simply not my business if someone else wants to raise their children differently.

My judgment on this subject had the same impact as a talk show I watched a few years ago in which stay-at-home moms sat on one side of the aisle and working moms sat on the other. I was heartbroken by the harsh things the moms said to each other. I didn't realize I was sitting in judgment, too, but since I thought highly of my own opinion, I felt righteous and justified. Today, I'm humbled by the judgment I found in my own heart. I pondered how many other instances I hurt people by my freely given opinion, when I could have kept it to myself unless asked for it.

What if we all listened more and talked less? Loved more and judged less?

I've heard from many moms who have chosen to have a career while they raise their kids. Their love is not less because they spend less time with their children. The flip-side for the stay-at-home mom is that some resent having to stay home. It might be better if these moms could work part-time. The important point here is, Mamas, choose as you feel led and don't worry about the judgment of others. If each of us were a little kinder to each other, despite having different opinions, we might remember that we're sisters, and we're on the same team. Believing we're on different sides of the aisle makes us forget that God's DNA flows through all our veins.

The common bond all moms feel at some point is guilt and the fear that they're missing it all. There are numerous instances in which our hearts are torn because of our intense love for our children, yet we can't protect them from the pain of their journey. I spent years holding on tightly to my children emotionally, begging God day and night to fix their struggles and keep them from pain. I had a death-grip on heaven's phone line daily. One day as I sat at a traffic light, yet again asking God to watch over my son at school and save him from trouble. In the middle of my request, I suddenly realized that I didn't believe my son is God's son, too. I didn't trust Him to have my son's back. I thought I loved him more than his heavenly Father, who created him. How humbled I was to realize I was stressing over how well God would take care of His child.

What if I trusted God to win my son's heart as He did mine? What if I didn't worry about my son's journey, instead, simply ask God to give him grace for the challenging lessons he'll experience and protection from the accuser who would seek to steal his peace?

When I listen, I learn. Many times, my opinions are established due to how I was raised. There are many varying opinions, and by listening, I might learn something new. The way we're taught isn't always best.

CHAPTER 14

love with wisdom

The most challenging thing about difficult people in our lives is to love them anyway. It's easy to love those who are lovable but challenging to love when it's not reciprocated. When people are difficult, usually, that's when they need love the most.

Many years ago, I felt like a dog on a tight leash with a friend. If I didn't check in with her every week, I'd receive the cold shoulder until I jumped through hoops again to make her feel cared for. This continued for a few years. I cared about her but was finding it increasingly difficult to be a friend. One day, I decided, I don't want to live like this for one more day. I'm going to quit being a friend in this way. I took all the pressure off myself and decided I would let her make the decision when she wanted to reach out to me. Much to my surprise, the dynamic completely changed, and this friend began to initiate conversation and take responsibility for our friendship.

No one asked me to be the accountable one. I took it upon myself because I believed I needed to take care of everyone else despite the cost. My relationship with this friend became healthy. When we lack wisdom in how we respond, we get used by others. It's not the other's fault—it's ours. When we love without boundaries, we set ourselves up to be used by others who lack boundaries.

Throughout my marriage, I found it difficult to find balance with my husband. I believed I needed to let him lead in all areas without questioning his decisions in our relationship. This pressure created imbalance to a great degree. I tried to follow as instructed, but I simply wasn't created to be a blind follower of another person. God created us male and female, and we differ greatly, but His Spirit within us does not see the differences—we're the same. I spent years trying to fit into the mold my church created for women, and one day the dam burst. In a serious discussion with God, I relayed to Him my intense struggle and that I'd rather live alone than continue as we were.

Again, I was surprised to find a defining moment at this crossroad in our relationship. Our relationship changed. I was, by my own beliefs, putting my husband in a position he didn't ask for. It was a difficult process for him to get used to, because it varied so drastically from previous years. It was incredibly difficult for him to suddenly get used to an equal partner, instead of a blind follower. I was quite defensive for the next few years as I sought footing in this new arena. I was easily offended when my husband challenged something I believed that differed from his beliefs.

With time and grace, little by little, I found my way to peace and confidence in my ability to know God. I no longer had to go through a father figure to tell me how it should be done.

The word love is flung about so easily, it often lacks substance. Love without wisdom allows lawlessness to abound. Those who abide in love are happy to live by the laws of the land without challenging them. It's those living in judgment and lawlessness who need laws. Love without wisdom causes us to want the same level of freedom for everyone, instead of realizing that those who don't abide in love will destroy what is good; they need to be governed by love with wisdom.

Jesus, while on earth, went about as He was led. He didn't heal everyone, but He healed everyone He met. There were needs as great then as they are today, but He simply walked where the Spirit led Him, touching all He encountered—wisdom with love at work.

Many times, we wonder how God could allow evil things to happen as they do. What I'm reminded of frequently is that it's the bittersweet result of freedom to choose. We want Him to make everything beautiful, but God doesn't push Himself on us. He loves us and invites us to agree with His way of seeing ourselves. We are free to partake of His vision for our life, but freedom to choose means evil will abound. Not everyone wants to partake.

Many times, we spend much time praying and asking God what He wants us to do. Much time is wasted by not utilizing our talents. What we do doesn't add to or take away from how God see us. We are made righteous by His Son. What if we started doing the things close to our heart and found that He'd given us the keys to our life path from the beginning? What if, instead of competing with others for validation, we begin to walk in the areas our hearts felt drawn to? What if we find out it's our path and our niche?

How many times have you heard, "What you feed grows?" If we believe this and begin to agree with God about the truth of who we are, we'll shift the focus from our faults and insecurities to seeing ourselves made whole by Him.

When we see ourselves through His eyes, we'll leave behind the need to be validated by others. We'll walk in confidence each day, because despite what others may think, we know our identity and we find peace in the ordinary, everyday things we do.

We're no more and no less than anyone else. Many times, due to our childhood experiences, we buy into the belief that we're less than others and of no importance. It's why we love to follow others. It's often why we buy into a certain religion because it makes us feel safe to have rules and regulations set out for us to follow. It seems dangerous to trust God with our hearts without someone on earth to keep us in line.

What if He holds your heart in His hands and knows exactly how to be enough for you? What if you can trust Him with your heart? What if He can speak to you by His Spirit, just as He did with Jesus and other important people you follow?

What if His wisdom resides within you and will guide you through life and show you how to love?

CHAPTER 15

purpose for
the dark places

As a little girl, I was incredibly timid and lived with intense anxiety. Many life events contributed to that anxiety.

I was terrified of the dark from a young age. While trying to go to sleep at night, my pulse would be so loud that I'd imagine it was a big, brown, grizzly bear coming to maul me. I'd squeeze my eyes shut, cover my head with the blanket, regardless of how warm the room was, and hope the blanket would protect me from the monsters that swayed and morphed around the room. I found it safer to close my eyes in the dark, lest I see the creatures around me.

Sexual molestation became a part of my life before I was old enough to express what was happening. I cried out for my mom. It occurred again a few years later, and with it came shame for the dirty, undeserving-of-love girl I felt I was. Due to how things were handled by my guardians, I decided it was up to me to protect myself. Anxiety peaked at night, and I learned soon that if I stuffed myself with food to the point of pain, I wouldn't feel quite as anxious.

With the stuffing of food came the widening of my waist and comments about my habits. It only served to pile more shame on top of how badly I felt about myself. I mocked the girl in the mirror for her weakness. I mocked her for how she chose to take care of herself.

I don't recall as a child, ever hearing a, "Good job, Katie!" I didn't have an adult voice to contradict the thoughts that lived in my head. I was shamed for the things I did that were deemed wrong. And for the first twenty-nine and a half years, the thoughts stayed locked up in my head, but they manifested themselves in my body's deteriorating health.

I was afraid of the God I was taught about. I believed Him to be a bogey-man who sat on His massive throne, ready to strike me down for all my evil deeds. There was hope of some gentleness due to my dad's example of talking to God as a person. But fear won over hope each time I found myself in a scary, unsure place.

I remember praying to God alone, while out walking. As young as aged ten, my heart desperately wanted to know my Creator. I didn't hear Him answer. I kept trying to be a good girl, despite my tendency to lie when I was afraid of punishment and for being dirty from hands that touched the places that should've been kept safe. Alas, predators abound, often in the form of those we trust most. Because they are so kind, we assume they are safe. The spirit of sexual abuse chooses its victims by their demeanor. It knows the ones who can be victimized and intimidated into silence.

I struggled for many years with the way my parents raised me. I struggled to forgive them for the intense, painful parts of my childhood and youth.

The tide changed gently and slowly when I had my own children. I realized I loved them fiercely, yet there were times when they talked of things that had crushed their little hearts that I never would have suspected. I had no idea these things would have left painful marks on their hearts. As these moments occurred, it helped me reflect on my parent's way of raising us and now view them in a new light. I processed the pain, beginning at the age of thirty, and continuing for the next ten years, culminating with my first book. I gradually came to know what mattered most was that my parents loved me to the best of their ability. They experienced abuse and intense pain and survived, and through their brokenness, they parented me.

When I saw their human-ness just as I saw my own through the eyes of my children, my perspective was transformed. They were no longer the giants in my view, but instead had become equals. I no longer demanded they be perfect, know all the answers, and take all the pain away that they inflicted on me. I allowed for weakness, pain, scars, and imperfection, realizing they loved me in the best way they were able to express it.

I am one of those moms who sought to parent perfectly. I felt emotionally neglected growing up, so I invested great effort seeing to the emotional needs of my children. I decided early on never to scream at my children, (my children still consider a slightly raised voice, yelling), to taste my words before I spit them out, and to never lie to them. Guess what? My children have as much pain as I had—it just looks different. I thought that because of the deficit I felt, I could fill their hearts so full, they'd never experience the feeling that they weren't good enough.

I've cried more in the last year concerning the struggles my children have experienced than any year leading up to this. I realize my children are going to have to work through their pain and frustrations with me, just as I had to with my parents, and they with theirs. The more grace I give my parents for being as they were, the more grace I can give myself to be as I am, trusting that someday, my children will arrive at the same place of peace.

We do love as we learn love. For most of us, that means we experienced abuse in some form, harsh and critical words, and heard comments such as, "you'll never amount to anything," "I wish you wouldn't have been born," or "You should be ashamed of yourself!" They are the words and deeds our parents were raised with. When we find peace with what was, we can do love differently. Love touched by grace binds up the wounds of the soul.

Being able to forgive our parents for the trauma and turmoil we experienced sets us free and, in turn, sets our parents free to do love differently. What if we can help our parents make peace with their parents by allowing God's love in us enable us to heal them?

What if the dark places you were entrusted with were to bring hope and healing to others? You know the depths of pain that should never have happened, but the curses that were handed down from generation to generation alighted at your door. What if through the intensity of the pain and your healing, you bring light to the darkest places of another? What if they find hope because they know you feel their pain? In making peace with the most terrible things you experienced, you extend that peace to the person next to you.

CHAPTER 16

she feels deeply

Over the past few years, I've come to realize that I will always feel deeply. I tried for the first thirty years to not feel. I practiced distancing myself when someone hurt me. I'd crawl into the shell I'd so carefully constructed so it would only open from the inside. I know I hurt my husband by keeping my heart from him when I felt vulnerable because his words or actions hurt me. It was the only way I knew to react.

A few years ago, I made a conscious decision to stay present when I was hurt, to hold the shell open, even when I wanted to retreat to the safety I'd always known. As you've probably guessed, I started getting lots of opportunities to practice my intention. I was far from perfect in this, but little by little, I began to trust my heart to feel the pain yet stay out there. I used to beat myself up for being such a weak person.

Today, I realize I feel deeply, and that's part of what makes me the strong woman I am. I feel the pain others feel and often pick up on the emotions people feel but don't express. When I'm at peace with this part of me, I thrive. When I'm hurt by things others do or say, I feel the pain, but I seek to understand things from their perspective, thus returning love when at times, I'm tempted to return fire.

When someone close to me doesn't support me as I'd hoped, it hurts, but I remind myself that it's okay. I'm not defined by someone else's support of the things I choose to do. I've so often heard things like, "If someone doesn't make time for you, don't waste time waiting for them." Or "If I'm important to my friend, they'll always make time for me." Many times, these statements are true, but when you look at it objectively, what if we're asking our friends to fill a spot they're not intended to fill? Many times, our interactions with those close to us come from a place in our heart we want filled, but those we love can't fill it.

When a friend hurts us, we're tempted to maintain distance, but the challenge is to keep our heart open anyway. Much of the time, we still respond to relationship challenges the same way we did as a child. "If you don't play what I want, I won't be your friend." We love with conditions to protect ourselves. The invitation in these moments is to love unconditionally, to let others love as they know how and seek to understand how they do love.

For many years, I expected my husband to love me in my language. When he didn't, my heart was crushed repeatedly. I love giving gifts and receiving them, but it's not my husband's thing. I even had him read the book on love languages, mostly to no avail, causing intense frustration and hurt for me. There were times I gave him a gift I'd put much thought into, and it didn't seem to mean anything to him.

For me, it was simple. I just needed him to buy me some little gifts here and there.

A few years ago, I made a conscious decision to notice how he does love. I knew it wasn't with gifts, but I did notice he worked hard to provide a good life for me and our children. He worked hard so I could be a stay-at-home mom. He's affectionate and makes it his personal mission to make me laugh. These are just some of the ways he shows love. When I notice and show appreciation for the way he does love, it brings out the best in him. My day is brighter because I'm feeling grateful for the way he does love, and I'm assured of his love. If I were to demand he love the way I want him to, I'd never be happy. Now, when he does bring me a gift, I receive it as a bonus token, not the whole of his expression of love.

This experience has helped me in other relationships. I'm practicing giving others room to love as they do, seeking to understand their way of expression instead of demanding they love the way I do.

Don't withdraw when others love with conditions. Be the one to love anyway. Be the one to show unconditional love, which means being vulnerable when you'd rather retreat. Know that most of the time, another's reaction has little to do with you and more to do with their way of being. In doing so, our hearts will get hurt at times, but isn't that the goal in life? To love even when it hurts? To love with our whole hearts? To learn to love without limits?

CHAPTER 17

passive aggressive

When we don't voice our needs, we constantly go about hoping those close to us will pick up on our needs and fulfill them. When our needs aren't noticed and met by others, we throw daggers in a backhanded way, but they're daggers all the same, leaving wounds where they pierce another's heart.

Kelsey was a vibrant middle-aged woman, mother of three beautiful children. From the outside in, it appeared she had everything, but her needs weren't being met; thus, those around her were frequently at the receiving end of her razor-sharp, cutting words.

In conversation with others, she'd frequently comment on something her husband failed to do for her or talked of how he just wasn't right, her solution was the one needed. For the casual observer, it may not have been obvious that she was hurting her husband, but if one noticed the closing of his eyes or the tightening of his lips, it was clear her comments caused him a lot of pain.

Kelsey would bring up scenarios in conversation of things that bothered her, talking about things she'd accomplished, hoping her husband would hear and appreciate her for her accomplishments. The bottom line is, there was nothing her husband could fix because her need for validation superseded any one person's ability to fulfill, except for the heart-shaped hole God created within her to fill with Himself. Her husband loved her to the best of his ability, but it was never enough until she received the revelation that God is her heart-filler. He is her identity.

Encouragement from a friend reminded Kelsey to look for the things her husband does right and tell him, showing appreciation for these things and speaking well of him to others. Her friend gently reminded Kelsey that making cutting remarks about her husband to others hurt him even if he didn't say anything. Kelsey thought her husband had everything together and his ducks were effortlessly lined in a row. She failed to notice he needed her approval too, and her words had the ability to cut so deeply.

In the culture I was raised in, I wasn't taught the importance of showing respect to my husband. Many times over the years, the comments I made to him, especially in the company of others, made him feel he was of little value to me. I loved him to the best of my ability, but I didn't realize how my sarcastic comments, my go-to deflectors, would affect him. Reading books on the differences between men and women opened my eyes to the power in a woman's words and how she can emasculate the man in her life by her treatment of him.

A man wants to please his woman. Many times, over the years, I've heard stories of how a man had a beautiful wife and family and threw it away for a fling with another woman. Frequently, the woman thought it was only for sex, but many times, the new woman showed him value and respected his opinions. While this by no means makes the man's decision right, it again points to the power a woman has. Much of the time, she's oblivious to it, often doing only what she watched her mom do.

Affairs go both ways, and I don't stand on any authority to say I know why everyone makes the choices they do, but since I'm writing for women, I'm sharing the female perspective. Although we've largely bought into the idea that it's a man's world, maybe, just maybe, if we stop and look at things from a different perspective, we'll realize that we've given our power away, groveling to be allowed to walk alongside men, striving to be equals, when all the while, we're powerful creatures, designed to lead in the arenas we have the privilege to create.

When we know who we are, we don't need to get others to notice our accomplishments and ask them to pat us on the back. We'll walk in confidence of our abilities, not competing with others, but fulfilling our own calling, our individual path. When we walk as such, we won't feel the need to compete with any man; instead, we'll realize we were created differently, and therein lies our super-power. We'll leave our unique imprint on the world and blaze our own path.

Being passive-aggressive is often the result of not having the courage to ask for what we need. We resent others for not knowing what we need; thus, sending jabs to hurt them in a roundabout way of expressing our pain, hoping against hope they'll get our subtle hints.

We lash out at those who do have the courage to ask for what they want. To go a step further, it is also why so many women, instead of supporting each other in taking new territory, cut each other down to make ourselves feel better. We feel envious of another woman's freedom, yet we're trapped by our own state of being. When a woman fails at a new venture, we secretly feel happy about her pain.

What if we each go after our dreams and support our sisters in their ventures at the same time? What if we cut ourselves every time we cut another? What if, instead of raging at men for making it a man's world, we instead see that we ourselves divide and conquer among our sisters? The fight is not with men, but with ourselves. It is up to us to move forward in life, remembering that we are woven from the same cloth. Similar DNA runs through our veins, regardless our color, differences in beliefs and where we live. We are first sisters, and therein lies our success.

CHAPTER 18

naturally nurturing

When I got married, I loved my husband with all my heart. What I mean by that is, I did my best to treat him well, be loving, cook for him, and do all the other things that go with housekeeping. When he had a problem with the way I did something, I changed the way I did it. I changed so much that the person I was on our wedding day disappeared with each passing day. The day came when I couldn't find me outside of my husband's identity.

Mandy got married to her high school sweetheart; they had two children and worked day after day to provide a life together. Her husband was critical of almost everything Mandy did. She kept adjusting at every turn, until one day, she realized she hated her life and felt hopeless that things could improve. She filed for divorce and set out to create a new life for herself. When I asked her if she kept her married last name, she exclaimed, "No, I had to get my identity back!"

Mandy's story is not unusual. I've heard from many women who found themselves near middle age and realized they didn't know who they were anymore. In our desire to nurture, we arrive at a place we never imagined we'd get to, not remembering who we were before we changed to become who we thought our husband wanted us to be.

Where does the blame lie in this? We could say it's the husband's fault because he criticized too much, or we could say it's the woman's fault because she gave up herself to make her husband happy. Placing fault doesn't fix a problem. What if we find the solution by asking ourselves who we were before we changed for our husband? Do we resent him for where we find ourselves? Could it be that we gave up who we were to keep the peace? We loved without boundaries and wanted to be accepted, so we didn't have the courage to say, "I like the way I do this." Or "Your way works for you and mine works for me." Or, "Sometimes my way is right too."

When we lack confidence in who we are, we're okay with feeling frustrated with others, but we get nervous when others are upset with us. We seek to please and appease to keep others happy at the expense of our own peace.

Karrie, a beautiful woman, wife, and mother of three children, handled everything life threw at her, making it look like a piece of cake. When her husband wanted something, he got it. Karrie had no voice for her own needs and when there was a disagreement between the two, she gave in to keep the peace. Day by day, the vivacious woman she was on her wedding day disappeared, until one day she looked and couldn't find the younger version of herself. What she saw was a mere shell of who'd she'd been, and her heart felt cold toward her husband.

The day Karrie realized she'd lost herself in her husband's identity, she began to react to his demands. Often, she reacted unkindly. She's been held under for so long, she couldn't bear another day of her husband's "my way or the highway" attitude. Her husband felt confused with his wife, who suddenly and without explanation turned away from his attempts to love her.

Just like Karrie, many of us who have been asleep to ourselves for a long time react with anger because we don't know who we are. Therefore, we can't simply express our wants and needs. We feel broken down. Our only way of expressing our emotions is in protest, much as a child who can't yet speak pushes someone away they don't want near them.

As Karrie processed her emotions, she gradually came to realize that her husband, while a naturally demanding person, wouldn't have treated her as he did if she'd spoken up from the beginning. Since Karrie gave in at every turn, her husband wasn't motivated to be thoughtful or considerate of her opinions.

Gradually, over time, Karrie began to command respect by asking for the things she wanted. Initially her husband protested dramatically, but when he realized her days of being a doormat for him were over, he became motivated to seek his wife's preferences. This process took a few years but were you to ask Karrie's husband today which version he liked better, he'd tell you he loves the woman who knows her own mind.

While Christians teach a man, as the Bible instructs, is to love his wife as Jesus loves the church, many times women believe they must blindly follow their husbands which creates an imbalance. I've known far too many women who've been doormats and resent their husbands because they become demanding bullies when their authority is unchecked. A husband is motivated to serve and please his wife when she knows who she is and walks confidently in her identity.

When we go back to the drawing board, we gradually find our footing again. Those we love will complain, and some will throw temper tantrums. I'm not just referring to children here, because sometimes they don't like this woman growing wings to be herself and the new confidence sprouting up within her. They were comfortable with the old way, and now they must respond differently. She no longer burns herself out to serve everyone else. She realizes she's worthy of being treated with respect, too. She evokes in others the desire to win her heart by serving her, as she serves others.

When we walk confident in our identity, we no longer feel the need to lash out at those we believe don't recognize our worth. We know they don't get to decide our worth. When we take our power back, remember what we're worth, we command respect by the way we conduct ourselves, not by ranting at others for not seeing it, but by quiet strength and confidence.

We still nurture, but we have balance.

CHAPTER 19

the power of the tongue

"Death and life are in the power of the tongue; and they that love it shall eat the fruit thereof." [1]

These words have been ever on my mind over the past two years. I spent most of my life being kind to others, but I spoke death over myself daily.

My life patterned itself after the words that filled my mind daily. I'm too fat, ashamed, guilty, a failure, and unworthy of love. Much of the time, when someone else said something that offended me, I projected on them the things I felt about myself. Regardless of their exact words, I heard it as the reel in my mind's eye showed it, which played and replayed in my mind.

How many times have you heard someone say, "But that's not what I meant!" or "That's not what I said." Yet you were positive the way you heard it was the way they intended it?

Each one of us hears differently. I remember as though it were yesterday, the day my granny Eva said, "But how can a piece of fabric keep you out of heaven?" Immediately, a light went on as I realized the material I wore on my head to keep my salvation, to keep me in right standing with God, would burn, were fire put to it. She said this in response to my questions concerning the issue I was contemplating at the time, whether to wear the head covering I was raised to believe was essential to get to heaven.

While that was a defining day in my life, I realized years later that she was trying to get me to see I was making a big deal out of nothing, and that I should just wear it. For me, it was a huge deal. I had spent my life with a covering on my head, to the point that when I'd wake up in the middle of the night to find my sleep kapp had come off, I rooted around in the covers until I found it. The words my dad spoke churned in my head as I desperately sought the kapp, "What if Jesus comes back in the middle of the night and you're not wearing your kapp?" My fear of this happening evoked tremendous trepidation. If He were to return in the middle of the night and my kapp wasn't on, I believed I'd go straight to hell.

As a teenager, I felt envious of my friends who spent hours without their covering on, their hair flowing freely as it dried after being washed. Not me—my hair was put up immediately after washing it, still wet. A friend commented one evening that it would be healthy for my hair if I'd let it hang free sometimes. I couldn't bring myself to tell her that for my own peace of mind, I had to keep my head covered day and night.

The things we are taught from our youth have tremendous impact on us. Many times, we believe things without questioning what we're taught. Many times, it causes division among us, each believing our belief to be the right one and assured all others have it wrong.

We spend a lot of time defending our position and our view of things until something earth-shattering happens to remind us just how many things don't matter.

The words spoken to us as truth become a part of the mantra playing in our minds, powerful enough to cause us to turn away from things that threaten our stance. Then one day, as our hearts open to the possibility that maybe what we thought was truth is simply one person's belief. The belief simply got turned into a religion for a whole fellowship to follow, thus, creating a system.

We hear the warning, "You'll go to hell if you leave." Issued to some people who consider leaving the religion of their birth and it has the power to halt a person's choice. It often keeps a person from leaving because they believe it. They'd rather live in misery with a tormented mind than have the certainty of spending eternity in hell. Again, the power of the tongue pervades over all else. Most of the time, only when a person is assured of their standing with God do they have the courage to leave the "church" and live in peace with their decision.

My husband chose at a young age to follow his convictions. His decision led him to a crossroad. He had to choose between God and family. He chose God and lost his family. Often with time, many families experience some reconciliation, and the words spoken in the heat of the moment soften as years pass by. I think many times, the words spoken are remembered by the person leaving much more clearly than the one who stayed. It can take time and grace to forgive the words.

My life is completely different than that of my youth, but I love my people and know that they live according to what they believe, as do I. I bless them in all their endeavors.

I used to struggle with feeling bitter towards the church of my teen years. It was such a difficult experience for me. But the gift that church gave me was the journey that led me to today. I'm richer for having known them. I'm grateful for the people who gave me the gifts they did, even if, for a season, those gifts were dark and painful for me. I bless them and wish them well.

God takes care of each one of us. It's not up to us to decide how others live. We are simply instructed to love our neighbors as ourselves. I say that from experience. I've spent so much time judging others according to my beliefs and found myself in a place of uncharted waters, suddenly bereft of direction. All my judgment did nothing for anyone except to speak death to them and in return, death to me.

Reflecting on the many times I've spoken from a place of judgment I had no authority to speak on has left me greatly humbled. I am reminded of the fact that when I judge others, I'm speaking critically, and that judgment returns to me. May I ever speak life and blessing to others. God in me speaks life always, for there's no death in Him.

CHAPTER 20

a champion for others

The sexual molestation I experienced as a little girl infiltrated every area of my life. I was marked by the spirit transferred to me by the offenders. I received the heaviness and shame they carried when the molestation occurred.

Held in the grips of the pain for many years, I unwillingly carried the shame it brought to me. I was able to see other girls who suffered as I did but I felt helpless to help them. I felt angry each time I saw the eyes of a predator, not by actions or words, but by recognizing the predator's look.

When I found healing from the stain that was part of my identity, the glasses I looked through became clearer. Having received healing from the pain and bitterness of the abuse and the way it was handled, I finally developed the ability to share my story without fear of judgment for what happened to me. I understood that even though the spirit this molestation operated in was handed down from previous generations, it stopped with me. It would go no further.

I became a champion for others, an ear for them to be able to voice their pain. I knew. I understood. While there are greatly varying degrees of sexual abuse, the shame the victims carry is the same. Believing oneself to be dirty, unworthy of love, they carry anger and rage just under the surface that often manifests itself in the form of self-sabotage. It may take the form of drugs, alcohol, excess food, or other coping methods. At worst, the victim becomes a predator, continuing to operate in the spirit brought on them by another's actions.

Seeking freedom from the heaviness I carried, just six months before my thirtieth birthday, I began to ask God for this to be my best year. By voicing that Intention, I wandered closer and closer to the carefully constructed walls I'd built for safety over the years. Yet, when I got too close to the dark corners of my heart, I'd quickly retreat to a safe distance, ever seeking to control my chaotic thoughts and emotions. I cried most days without resolution.

My thirtieth year arrived, and I felt at peace with the new milestone. Many things in my life were good, especially since I'd gotten so used to using food as a band aid for all the upheaval I silently struggled with. It took almost ten more years to be finally free of the baggage. During this journey, I found God in so many of the places where I thought He'd left me alone. His hand on my life over the years was there. I just didn't recognize it.

The freedom I found was sweeter yet than the peace I had found years earlier. The journey is what worked love and compassion into my heart. The long, broken road brought me to a love I didn't know existed. The DNA running through my veins was enveloped in clean blood, blood that told of a love so great, a Father submitted His Son to enter my darkness. My Father who loved me so much, He had paved the way years earlier, I just didn't know it. This love, when experienced, releases restoration blood through the veins of every one of His children who will receive it.

I could have held onto the pain, but His gentle coaxing led me to understand the freedom from it was infinitely better. Releasing the long-held pain, well-hidden in the confines of my heart, was the starting point for my true identity.

Where I'd wrestled with shame and guilt, I realized it was no longer mine to carry. He had paved the way for me to simply receive the all-encompassing gift of His love and let Him claim the dark places He'd already claimed thousands of years ago. Therein lies our freedom—the realization that He took our shame and gave us grace instead.

When replaced with love, all the pain one carries gets turned into love that touches others and offers hope of a life without shame. Love is everything. It doesn't demand anything. It simply invites us at every turn to participate in the redeemed life He's provided.

For so many years, I hobbled along in duress under the weight of the dark things. When melted away, I was able to become a voice for the abused. When we know we need not be ashamed, we stand tall and confident in the love we know is Him. Knowing His love enables us to live free and love freely. We then invite others to partake of His love when the light in us reflects the tiny spark of hope in theirs.

How sweet a gift it is, to no longer carry the weight that hounded me for most of my life. How amazing the gift of a shame-free soul, growing ever-more open to be filled increasingly with the essence of the One who was designed for it from the beginning.

He makes the things that were as though they are no longer. He turns mourning into joy and gives lightness of spirit to the downcast and carriers of darkness, helping them to see the darkness wasn't theirs to carry. He had lifted the darkness before we alighted on this earth, before we took our first breath. Is it not, then, the most effective lie for humanity to believe that we're separated from Him, and that He's an angry Father waiting to hurt us when we stumble or choose unwisely?

What if, instead, we see the great love He has for us and the anticipation He feels waiting for us to accept it. He patiently waits for us to realize the life He has provided. All we have to do is receive it. What if we were not ashamed but boldly agreed with Him that He sees us as flawless, through His Son who paid for even the darkest spot within us.

Taking our place alongside each other, we can remember that we're each His creation, siblings to each other. In realizing we're siblings, we do away with the division we buy into from the father of lies. Instead of believing we're on different sides and must fight to defend our stance, what if we realize we're out of many, one? We then become champions for each other.

CHAPTER 21

the truth

When we see new truths, we want to enlighten the whole world with our newfound perspectives. Many times, our excitement overwhelms others' receptiveness. Some see the truth, and others reject it. This often creates challenges and pain for both parties.

Growing up in religion, I learned to expect everyone to believe the same way. When someone left the church, it was often whispered amongst the church people, "They've found a strange belief." This immediately set a wall of division between the one who left and the ones remaining. To protect their beliefs, the church often chose to excommunicate the person who left, lest others follow suit.

It seems we human beings are inclined to create boxes to live within to feel safe. We believe we must have a belief system. When our beliefs are challenged, we hold faster to the things we believe, closing our ears, lest we hear something new and are faced with a decision to stay the same or change, no longer innocent. Closing our minds creates a safety net for us, enabling us to hold on to the teachings of our youth and keep the world at bay.

Being so open to new truths that they impact the place you're living in is scary territory when you've been within the safety net all your life. You can always find someone to agree with your beliefs, but what if allowing your beliefs to be challenged opens your eyes to truth you didn't know existed? It is indeed quite scary to be this open. In many religions you're warned of this constantly. We're taught that we must listen to the belief system pre-set by the church we've decided to agree with. It makes us feel safe to stay within the confines of the rules and beliefs, making it easy to judge others who don't agree.

What if we were to open our hearts to the One who created us and made a place for His Spirit to abide within, to teach us all things? What if He's given each of us the knowledge of how to live? *"But the anointing which ye have received of Him abideth in you, and ye need not that any man teaches you: but as the same anointing teacheth you of all things, and is truth, and is no lie, and even as it hath taught you, ye shall abide in him."*[1]

While our tendency is to build boxes to keep ourselves and each other in place, what if we were to experience a love so immense, we no longer needed to hold onto walls to keep the world outside? What if we find He is able to keep us by simply entrusting our hearts to Him? If He's the one who created us, did He not give forethought to our needs and put within us, who carry his DNA, the ability to know His voice from all others?

There are many voices, and they often cry loudly, pulling us in various directions. Fear is the loudest of them. Is it not fear that propels us to stay within the boxes we've built? Is it not fear that holds us in place when we feel drawn to look over the walls of the box?

The fear of what might happen has held me in my box many more times than not. It's a scary thing to venture outside, but what if we find His voice within is stronger than any other? From the quietest place in the heart, His voice leads and directs, even though other voices may say that's not what we were taught.

A few years ago, Carol experienced freedom from the shackles of shame that had held her from youth. She was incredibly excited and wanted her friend Emily to see the truth, too. Despite her best efforts, Emily refused to see the truth and insisted on remaining behind her wall of fear and shame. This created frustration for Carol and stimulated her to preach at Emily day in and day out about the lies she was believing about herself. If she could simply see the truth Carol had discovered, Emily would find the same freedom and happiness Carol had found. The more Carol pushed, the more Emily resisted.

One day, while listening to a pastor share on the merits of loving others right where they are, Carol's heart melted. She realized she'd been demanding Emily come to the truth as she herself saw it and have the same experience she did. When Carol saw that her truth might look different than Emily's truth, her heart softened. She thought back over all the times she'd been challenged by others for believing things that didn't line up with their beliefs.

Carol realized that each person's journey to God looks different. We each see Him according to our life experiences. While we can be taught how to be a Christian, it doesn't hold water when we're asked to stand without any buffers of the teachings we were instilled with. According to the verse mentioned earlier in this chapter, God's goal isn't for us to be taught how to be a Christian; instead He desires each of us to know Him intimately through a deeply personal relationship.

Because there are so many different religions, all of whom believe theirs is the correct one, is it not then glaringly obvious that God's design for each of us to know Him individually is most important when approaching a relationship with Him? Does it not suggest that His word is to be made life by His Spirit within us, rather than by the interpretations of man? Teachers can enlighten us and open our eyes to truth, but it should agree with the Holy Spirit within us. Otherwise, we latch onto another person's understanding of who God is. What if we allow the teachings of fear and judgment to be stripped away and trust the Father who created us to show us truth? Are we able to trust Him that much?

His love, to me, is truth. He is the embodiment of love. His love has convicted me of my righteousness in Him far more effectively than the hard teachings of my youth. The teachings of my youth made me afraid of Him, trying to hide the dark places in my heart. By allowing Him access, His love shone through the broken places in my heart, bringing light to the darkest corners, and leaving in its wake love-filled cracks—whole, peaceful, and complete.

CHAPTER 22

joy in the journey

It's Sunday evening, and we're dreading Monday because a new work week begins. We grudgingly go through the work week, growing more excited as Friday nears, just to start the process all over again for next week—day in and day out, month after month, year after year, until we arrive at retirement age, waiting to die.

What about all the moments during the work week? How many life-changing moments did we miss because we had our head down obsessing about the daily grind? What if we paused and decided to look at things differently? For a few minutes, think about the millions of people who'd give anything to have the life we are blessed with. There are so many who work each day, scrounging enough together to have one small meal if they're lucky.

What about the skills we could develop, the classes we could take, the new things we could learn? There are so many opportunities awaiting us if we'd only take time to color outside the lines.

There are moments when life is crazy, and you literally need to put your head down and brace against the wind, such as in the busy season of motherhood or other caretaking responsibilities. I'm not talking about these seasons, but rather those when we have time to develop skills with subjects we're interested in. Instead, often we distract ourselves until it's time to do the next fun thing, rather than be purposeful with our lives.

We might be planning a trip somewhere for vacation, so we start counting down the days, just waiting for the vacation to commence. What about the days in-between? What connections did we miss in the meantime?

What about the journey?

I've spent way too much time holding my breath until I arrive at a new destination—the next youth group event or the next lunch with friends.

We live in a country that allows us to choose any career we want. We get to follow any path we choose, yet, we somehow find ways to make other people responsible for our inability to take new territory.

I spent years frustrated with my husband because he didn't want the same things I did, mistakenly believing he stood in my way. Yes, there are times when a husband really does stand in a woman's way, dictating what she's permitted to do. This is not right. That woman must find her way to freedom also.

I'm speaking for those who are taught certain things from youth and don't question their way of being. Had I not been too afraid that God would strike me down if I were to challenge my husband on things I disagreed with, I would've realized a lot sooner that he wasn't in my way. Leaning on the teachings I was raised with made it quite convenient to blame him, until life got so miserable I was willing to challenge absolutely everything I'd been taught just to find clarity in the confusion.

I think herein lies much of the struggle for us women. We've bought into the system we were taught. We live frustrated, and when we see other women step outside the system, rather than seeking to understand, we resent them and lash out at them. We continue to allow it, all the while blaming men and others who refuse to conform, while we sit on our self-righteous high-horse, saying we'd never make the choices "those" women are making.

What if we were to admit we're ashamed of our lack of education and skill development and feel trapped by a system we feel we're too old to escape? What if we admit we are worried about what others, who have chosen conformity, would think if we follow long-buried dreams?

The little girl you used to be is still in there. It's never too late to become who you wanted to be. What would change, were you to give voice to the dreams of your youth? Would you be more optimistic for young girls who talk excitedly about their future, instead of thinking to yourself, "Wonder how long it will take for her feet to hit the ground?" Or you might say, "Be realistic—what you want is too difficult, so choose something that's possible."

How many of our responses to our sisters come from a place of jealousy and envy because we believe life passed us over? What if we have the life we have because of the choices we made? Regardless of the reason for our current situation, we get to choose each day how we respond to life. We can be angry and bitter, or we can see each day as an extraordinary opportunity to see tiny miracles in our ordinary lives.

Choosing gratitude changes everything. Right here, right now, we get to decide how we live, regardless how those close to us choose to live their lives. How many times have we used the excuse, "I'd like to dream, but this person in my life keeps me from going after my dreams."

Are we believing in a fairy tale? Do we secretly believe we must wait for someone to hand us our dreams and give us permission to go after them? Is that why we're angry with our place in life?

What if we choose kindness? What if we choose peace? When one of us is struggling, instead of dishing out judgment, we should freely offer words of encouragement and affirmation.

Recently, I was able to help a young mom for a few hours when her babies were sick. It was so much fun to clean for her, knowing I'd been in her shoes not so long ago. I remembered the boost I received when someone helped me out. This mom had asked me to drop something in her mailbox because she thought her house was too messy and was embarrassed for me to see it. I assured her, it would be my pleasure to help.

I understand why she felt afraid or ashamed to let me see her house—not because it was as dirty as she thought it was, but because of my experience. I knew what it was to be gossiped about because of housekeeping skills. In the culture I grew up in, everything was done with the anticipation that another woman in the church would judge if it wasn't done to certain standards. Everyone sought to portray the persona of perfection. If a woman wasn't neat in her housekeeping, the whole community knew it. Do we really want to live with this kind of treatment toward each other? Are we not our sister's keeper?

What if we'd realize that the way someone keeps their house or dresses themselves or lives their life, doesn't affect how much they're loved? What if we focused on each other's hearts instead of their actions? What if we were to be about our Father's business of loving others and lifting them up when they're down, instead of standing on our soapbox, making sure others know we do things better? Could it be we're ashamed of the things hidden in our hearts and are afraid others may see inside, noticing how broken we really are?

What if we were to remind ourselves who we are and whose we are, filling the void that creates in us the need to gossip about others? What if we were to admit we don't have it all together, and we need a little grace too? Might we be a little bit kinder? Love a little deeper? Have a little more peace?

May we remember each day to be present. May we all pay attention to the little things and notice the tiny miracles. Has it not been said, "Someday we'll realize the big things really were the tiny, everyday moments?" If we're present for the tiny moments, we'll notice the beauty in them and live happier lives, loving others instead of competing with them. We know we'll eventually get to our destination but realize, if we rush, we'll miss out on the many joys of the journey.

CHAPTER 23

on your own

From the moment we take our first breath, we desire to be loved, held and cared for. However, most of us are raised with dysfunction to some extent. It is in this place that we learn how to ask for love. When raised with dysfunction, we often seek love in unhealthy ways.

Sometimes, we measure our worth by the status of our relationships. One of the most important things for us to learn is the ability to be on our own, without being in a romantic relationship.

Having a few friends who've been single for most of their lives, the comment I've most often heard from them is the pressure they feel when they don't have a man in their lives. People make all kinds of comments about their biological clock ticking and the fact they're not getting any younger. This is just one area where unsolicited advice hurts others.

When one relationship ends, regardless how broken our hearts feel, most immediately jump into the next relationship. We don't give ourselves time to mend or reflect on what happened or what we could do differently next time.

I find that regardless of our experience, we still have this starry-eyed view of love. We expect the man of our dreams to be our knight in shining armor and intuitively know how to meet all our needs. We start the relationship by giving all of ourselves. There are things that bother us in the relationship, but we brush them aside because we're in love. Time passes, and we wait with great anticipation for him to pop the question. When he does, we commence with planning our dream wedding.

As we get closer to "I do," things continually pop up, but instead of addressing the issues, we say, "You just wait until I marry him—I'm going to put my foot down." Or "He's going to find out what I think once we're married!" Or we spend all our dating time hiding who we really are, afraid the guy wouldn't go through with the marriage if he really knew us. We somehow think happily-ever-after is in the marriage. Once the guy marries us, we think he must love us, so we intend to show our true colors then.

The important thing to remember is, the man you marry will have just as much baggage to unpack as you do. No man can fulfill the void created to be filled by God. When we see that a relationship with a man is designed to complement our lives instead of complete us, we'll have a better life experience. When we find that no human relationship can provide the ultimate fulfillment, we'll seek God and give Him room to reveal His heart to us. We will be amazed at the transformation this creates in us.

If we were encouraged from a young age to go after our dreams and begin to build the life we want, our life partner would find us as we're building our castle. Many women tell me they are impatiently waiting and putting their life on hold for the man who's going to sweep them off their feet and live with them happily-ever-after,

On the flip-side are the women with the big chip on their shoulder who have decided they'll pick a man they can control. While understandable, it doesn't work long-term, since the man will learn to hide himself from the woman, and she'll find he's a dull bore.

Whatever situation you find yourself in, know this: until you fill the part meant to be filled with His Spirit, you'll find relationships repeatedly coming up short. Pay attention to the things you're drawn to and find fulfillment in the things God gifted you with. Build your skills with practice. Live fully. Take the time to let God heal the pain from your youth. The man and or others who will enrich your life will come, and you don't need to put your life on hold for someone else to make your dreams come true.

If a relationship ends, take time to let your heart mend. Blaming your ex for all your problems may seem like the solution, but if you begin another relationship without fixing the broken pieces within, you'll find yourself, a few years later, in the same situation with a different person.

When we rely on someone else to make our dreams come true, we give our power away. Others' dreams are different from ours. God gifted us with unique talents to develop so we can leave our own stamp on the world and those we love.

Rosanna, a lovely young woman, had her whole life in front of her, yet she couldn't bear to be single. She jumped quickly into relationships, one heartbreak after another. She couldn't imagine a life without a man to fulfill her. Each break-up left more pieces scattered on the ground behind her. Continually, she expected the man to make her dreams come true. In each relationship, she allowed the man to set the tone and make the rules, even the ones she desperately hated, giving in so she wouldn't be left on her own.

Rosanna lived in a perpetual state of feeling used and abandoned because each guy was unable to fill the deep void or dull the pain she hid deep within. Were Rosanna able to pause, she would have found that she could be whole on her own. Instead of hustling for her own worthiness, she would have found peace with the pain and realized she was whole and worthy just as she was, as a daughter of God.

There is a relationship designed for each one of us unlike any other. We may be taught all sorts of different things, but the common bond we have is this: God created us because He desired to have a relationship with each one of us. When we seek to know Him, regardless the length of time it takes, we'll find a relationship that supersedes all others—a relationship that fulfills our deepest needs and creates in us peace and rest with what is. After that, any human relationship is an added blessing and a contribution to our lives, not the basis for completion.

CHAPTER 24

woman, know yourself

Knowing who we are and educating ourselves, empowers us to live responsibly and helps us create the life we want. No woman should feel like she is at the mercy of others and helpless to change her situation.

In receiving feedback from many stay-at-home moms, finances prove to be a point of contention. I've heard many men who were the sole breadwinner in a relationship complain that the woman in his life spent all his money. There's a balance to be found. There are men who don't realize the cost of living, especially if the woman does all the grocery and clothes shopping. But there are also instances where a woman, not realizing how finances work, spends money as though it were in endless supply. This creates intense stress for the man responsible for her and the family's well-being.

When you demand the things you want, your man might do his best to give it to you but try to put yourself in his shoes. What if you were the one responsible for providing the income for your family and your spouse didn't understand what it takes, spending everything that comes in, leaving barely enough for the bills to be paid? I realize in some relationships the woman handles the finances and the husband is the one who overspends, and that's for a different book.

When we educate ourselves and know how to take care of the details, our self-respect increases. We'll alleviate the stress created by our overspending and we won't fight over money every month thereby restoring peace.

Educating yourself about finances puts the power of your future into your hands and gives you the ability to build the life you want instead of leaving it up to someone else. That way, you don't have to live frustrated, feeling your husband doesn't love you enough to give you what you want or doesn't want you to be happy. I don't know a man who doesn't want to make the woman in his life happy. When we work as a team and know the ins and outs of what it takes to make a living, we set ourselves up for success and won't live with resentment and conflict.

Of course, there are times when the man in your life may be burdened with pain from his youth and is unable to dream with you. It may seem difficult to have hope for a brighter future, but by knowing the important facts yourself, you might inspire him to dream with you and build a future together you'll both be proud of.

A woman at peace with herself is one of the most impacting creatures on the planet. When you love who you are, you'll move mountains. There may be bumpy roads in your relationship initially, but there isn't a man on earth who doesn't want to please and win the heart of a happy-with-herself woman.

Knowing yourself equals empowering yourself. Have you considered that the most restricted women on earth are the ones who are forbidden from getting an education? They are strictly bound to serve their man with no means of escape.

Many religions are set up to have the man lead and the woman follow, which is often the basis for not educating women. Today, we have the freedom to do anything a man does. Some things don't serve us well, such as trying to compete with men. We should remember we were created differently, and our strength is not in competing with men, but in knowing ourselves, realizing we have unique strengths men don't have and living within those strengths.

Another area of great importance is for women to know we're beautiful just as we are—that's one of our superpowers. The trend in today's world is to be super skinny. This creates havoc for us when we try to fit that mold. We are all varying shapes and sizes. We weren't all created to look the same. We live in a world where social media overshadows much of our lives. Perfectly airbrushed models grace the covers of magazines on the newsstands at the grocery store to constantly make us aware of our shortcomings.

Comparing ourselves to those standards, we will feel pressure about the shape of our bodies or our way of housekeeping and parenting. Many of us no longer walk with confidence and internal wisdom handed down generation to generation about the ways of taking care of our bodies and our children. We rely on others to tell us how to take care of ourselves.

What if we women took our power back and realized we get to choose what the world sees as beautiful and train our children to see what true beauty looks like? Why have we given ourselves away, allowing others to decide if we are beautiful or not? Our daughters are currently at the mercy of an unreachable goal of perfection.

This reminds me of the time my sister went on a trip to a third-world country when she was in college. The confidence the women had in this country had a lasting impact on her. It wasn't that any of the women met a standard of perfection; it was that they walked with confidence. They didn't walk around hoping others found them acceptable by a certain beauty standard. They felt beautiful; thus, they were beautiful. They didn't spend time criticizing imperfect parts of their bodies; instead, they loved their whole bodies.

This is a great example of women knowing who they are and walking in it. A woman who knows herself doesn't walk timidly, hoping others approve of her. She walks with her head held high, knowing she's loved and comfortable in her own skin. She commands respect and freely loves others, allowing them to become their own version of beautiful and confident.

Educate yourself. Allow the wisdom God instilled within you to lead you in all your decisions. Surround yourself with sisters who are there to support your journey to independence, those who will love you and have your back. Don't give room for criticism from those who don't know themselves to keep you in conformity. Freedom for women comes from women. We take our place and walk confidently in the way of our goals and dreams. There will always be naysayers, but instead of beating up men and other women who disagree with us, instead of blaming them for our inability to lead, let us walk according to our God-given calling to be strong, confident women, building each other up as we find our place and leave our mark on the world and those we love.

CHAPTER 25

helping the unwilling

Cassie is a beautiful young woman with much potential, yet she lives in a state of constant upheaval. She experienced abuse by a trusted family member and spent many of her teen years in and out of centers for abuse programs. Unfortunately, this experience didn't create solutions for Cassie; instead, it enabled her to learn how to manipulate others into giving her what she wanted. Whenever things don't go as Cassie wants, she says, "I just don't want to live anymore." Or "I just want to die."

Cassie believes she needs a man in her life. When one relationship ends, within days, she's connecting with a new man. Within a few weeks, she's in a relationship and talks of loving her new boyfriend with all her heart. She believes herself to be of such little worth that she'll give in to any demands her new boyfriend makes. She is desperate for his approval.

I was approached by a mutual friend and asked to lend an ear to Cassie. After a few weeks, I realized Cassie would come to me for advice, but when she didn't like my answer, she'd go to our mutual friend. If she liked her answer, I wouldn't hear from Cassie for a few weeks. When she liked my answer, I'd hear from her daily. By interacting with a number of counselors, she learned the language they spoke and used it to manipulate others into seeing things her way. It has proven a great disservice to Cassie and those who had tried to help her.

Cassie wants someone to do the hard work for her. What I mean by hard work is this: Cassie wants love, freedom, and happiness, but she wants someone else to guide her step by step instead of choosing to take care of herself. If anything proves challenging, she wants to harm herself and quit living. Cassie is the result of a dysfunctional upbringing, and it's easy to understand why she copes as she does. But as an adult, who's going to change her ways, if not her?

I can give Cassie advice, but if she doesn't want to know God for herself and find healing for the things done to her, she will always limp along. The effects of the abuse will remain a part of her identity keeping her from her best life.

For many years, I was a magnet for people like Cassie. I would buy into their story of abuse and carry their pain for them, enabling them to stay in an arrested state of development. By God's grace in my life, I'm compassionate and willing to be a listening ear and pray. However, I will no longer support people who choose to stay in dysfunction unless I see that they want to be free of it. I believe it to be my responsibility.

When you want to talk about who you are in Christ, focusing on your true identity, I'll be your biggest fan. Believing the identity life wrote on your slate will only serve to tell both of us that it's hopeless for you to live a victorious life.

A few years ago, a friend called me. She was struggling to find peace for a situation in her life. As our conversation continued, my friend began to rant about how badly God let her down and how He keeps leaving her high and dry. This had happened more than a few times throughout our friendship. I had always listened and allowed her to rant as she pleased, but this time, anger rose up within me. This woman was raging about my best friend. I could no longer listen as she hurt the One who'd loved me, rescued me, and filled my heart with the greatest love I've ever known. I stopped her mid rant and stated, "I can't listen to you speak of my friend this way, He's the best thing that's ever happened to me, I simply can't be a part of this."

In shock, after a long, awkward pause, my friend mumbled a half-hearted apology, and said she was having a hard time and was sorry I had to be the one to hear about it. She put the responsibility on my shoulders by letting me know she was struggling, and I was refusing to help her. I put an end to my help that day. I couldn't help her stay in her place of dysfunction.

I didn't hear from my friend for over a month. At times, I thought about trying to soften the blow. I was sure she felt hurt from my response, but each time I wanted to do something, I didn't feel any peace to proceed. I felt encouraged to let things be.

Over time, our friendship took on a new form. The important detail to note is this: I have no problem when someone is angry at God. I've found myself in many angry conversations with God because I didn't understand why He was acting a certain way. There have been times while telling Him exactly how frustrated I was with Him, my eyes suddenly opened to new truths. I realized He had to be as

He was because I was trying to see truth through the eyes of the teachings of my youth, instead of knowing truth by His Spirit. Each time, I sheepishly apologized and felt His smile and gratitude that His beloved agreed with Him, yet again.

When my friend was willing to see truth according to how God sees her, after the storm, fresh life burst forth. Her mind was freed of still more lies, replaced with the light of His countenance, which enabled her heart to expand with His love for her.

My part in our friendship was to quit supporting my friend's demands that God be what she thought He must be. By my obedience, one more avenue dried up which had enabled her dysfunctional behavior.

I experienced intense discomfort in standing up to my friend as I had. It was difficult for us both, yet I was a better friend when I challenged her dysfunction. In the past, I would have quietly listened until the conversation was through, then unloaded the heaviness to someone else because I'd find it too difficult to bear a moment longer. Is it not being the better friend when I address complications with you instead of allowing your dysfunction to continue?

It's challenging to be completely honest with others because there are many times when others won't receive it well, but true friendship asks for transparency. As my friend, you'll be assured that when I give it to you straight, you'll know I'm truly in your corner.

CHAPTER 26

challenging your beliefs

How much time have you spent defending your beliefs? Are you open to a new way of thinking, or do you hold onto the teachings of your youth, lest you be deceived?

There have been many times when I heard whisperings that challenged my stance on an issue. I'd try to cover my ears because the whispers were scary and uncomfortable. They threatened my cozy existence.

A few years ago, I heard a whisper in my heart to make some decisions concerning my future. I kept ignoring it, asking God to take the responsibility from me. I felt it was too difficult. The choices I needed to make would create some uncomfortable moments with people close to me. I kept putting the decision off, until one day when the decision was made for me. It was an extremely painful experience, and my relationship with some was forever altered, forcing me to take the step I'd been ignoring.

Had I made the challenging decision when I was impressed to do so, it would have been much less painful. I was afraid of how much my relationship would change and how I might offend others by my decision. I regretted ignoring the prompting I felt.

The challenge put to me was to realize that if I resisted making the changes needed, I'd have to one day look at my eighty-year-old self in the mirror and admit I had chosen to live a life less than I was capable of just to keep some people happy. I would have chosen to live half-heartedly; thus, the life I was meant to live went unlived, the box of gifts and talents returned to God, unopened and unused.

The painful experience that resulted from my inability to change evoked in me the intense desire to live my best life now, today, every day. I don't want to live half-heartedly; instead, I want to utilize each gift I've been given and be an inspiration for others to live their best life instead of encouraging them to just wait for the weekends.

The beautiful gift is, today is never too late to start. While making life choices that forge new paths instead of staying on the comfortable, predictable path, we meet new people and leave a lasting impact, with both of us forever changed.

Surround yourself with a few friends who encourage you to live fully. Be the one who encourages your friends to go the distance. How sad would it be to return the talents you were given, unused, knowing the world missed out on what you were sent to give and the mark you were created to make?

What if God's Spirit within you was designed to keep your heart? What if you didn't need to fear being led astray and making the wrong decisions? What if you made some wrong decisions, but He was faithful to bring you full circle, allowing the wrong steps you took to be an enriching lesson that served a greater purpose?

How small are our minds when we live within the confines of the things we were taught and shut out all others? We human beings seem to crave walls and boxes to feel safe in, but how often do those walls cave in and suffocate us? Desperate for fresh air, unable to bear the confines any longer, we knock down the walls, our hearts open to a new and different way.

Think of all the inventions we benefit from today. Had the inventors remained intent on staying in the world as it was, they would never have created the things that have impacted the world. Had they been too afraid to challenge the original way of doing things, they wouldn't have discovered what they were capable of. In the same way, when we close our ears to avoid being challenged for what we believe, we might miss out on some of the incredible freedoms we get to enjoy.

When I consider God, who created this incredible world and all of us with our individual blueprint, I imagine His disappointment when we go through each week waiting for the weekend to live. I imagine He's intently waiting for us to open our hungry hearts to understand Him in a new way and anticipating the new things we'll create with our unique voice and talents.

What if we were to trust His voice within us to the extent that we threw off the cloak of safety we've wrapped ourselves in and took bold, new steps? What if, instead of waiting for Him to plop our purpose in our laps, we did the things we are interested in and created new life?

The analogy I think of most often is this: can you imagine how you'd feel each day, were your child to ask, "What should I create today,

Mom?" Or "What do you want me to be?" Doesn't it make your heart glad when your child gathers the toys and blocks you've given them and creates something they're so proud to show you? Isn't that how they discover new abilities?

Doesn't it make sense then, that God's heart is glad when we build on the gifts we've been given and become adept at those talents, instead of waiting day after day, asking Him, "God, what should I do with my life?" Or "What would you have me build?"

Could it be, He's just as excited at the things we invent and create as we are with the things our children create? When we make a wrong turn, He'll direct us back to the right path. With His voice speaking within us, He'll give us wisdom to know what's true and what isn't.

What might you be capable of if you allow yourself the freedom to try new things? What if the situations you find yourself in are within your choice? Don't resent others and God because you feel stuck. What if He's waiting for you to build on what He's given you? What if, in allowing your tightly-held beliefs to be challenged, you find your whole life open in front of you? Oh, the places you'll go!

CHAPTER 27

us versus them

From the day I was born, I belonged to a church that taught we were "the church." They didn't always say those words, but if someone decided to leave the church, they were considered wrong for their decision. Each step along the way of my journey through life, I belonged to 'the church', until I didn't anymore.

With the church I belonged to as a teenager, the teachings were intense, and I served God with all my might. Stirred up after each revival meeting, I buckled down and served God even harder—that is, until I failed to tell the next person I met the good news that Jesus came to save them. I was then plunged into the depths of despair, condemned because I'd failed God yet again. I couldn't wait for the next revival meeting to have my slate wiped clean again.

I used to think if anyone visited our church and didn't return, they simply weren't willing to accept God's truth, but more accurately, it turned out to be our version of God's truth. I had no idea that the judgment I lived under was too heavy a load for some to carry, and as it turned out, it was too much for me as well.

Gradually, God found ways to open my heart to understand there was a better way. The first time I realized there was a better way was when I visited a small country church and responded to the altar call as I'd done countless times before in my desperate search for God. But this time was different. I felt warm, liquid love cover my heart and replace the harsh judgment I carried. I suddenly realized I was like every person who'd ever walked this earth. I was no better than anyone else, and my church wasn't "the church." Instead, we were a part of the whole, seeking to know the Father who gave us breath, and whose blood flowed through our veins.

Little by little, day after day, my heart began to understand that I'm my brother and sister's keeper. I'm out of many, one with each person on this earth. It doesn't matter what color differences our skin has, what features vary or what languages differ—we share similar DNA. The Creator of the universe is the God who gave breath to Adam and each one of us. He followed through the many generations to me. I have come from a mixed blend of people, cultures, and languages.

What if our greatest strength in unity will come from realizing this truth? How many of us allow prejudices to keep us apart? We stick with what we were taught and decide our way is true, and our way is best. We spend so much time being afraid we'll get deceived instead of living life, palms open, palms up, trusting our Creator to guide us with His wisdom.

What would there be to separate us, were we to realize we come from the same source? What if we're all His children with some just not realizing it yet? How differently would we treat each other if we all knew we're really the same—no more, no less than anyone else, but the same.

What if we chose to approach those who believe differently than we do with an open heart, giving them a chance to share their hearts? I expect we'd find we agree about a lot more things than we disagree.

The last election was filled with many devastating moments. We listened to the hateful words spewed by people who supposedly love each other. Because we believe we need two sides, we make our brothers and sisters our enemies, forgetting we're out of many, one.

How many times have we heard the phrase, "Turn off the news and love your neighbor"? In the middle of a devastating natural disaster or death in the family, we are so quick to lay all differences aside and help in whatever way needed, effortlessly remembering we're out of many, one.

What if we were to lose the white-knuckled grip on our long-held beliefs and prejudices and, with an open heart, love our family, our whole family? What if we knew a love so great as to create in us the ability to see past all barriers we've erected and simply love one another?

Is it simply buying into the lie that we're all different, speak different languages and believe differently, that makes us judge others? What if it's not up to us to decide who's right and who's wrong? I'm not here to be politically or theologically correct—I'm here to love you, my family. And when you've forgotten who you are, I want to tell you of a Father's love so great that He sent us love in a package measurable for us. He gave His Son to die for us—a death that took the place of all our deaths, thereby, giving the gift of life eternal.

We couldn't believe an angry Father who thought we deserved to die could love us more than an earthly parent can love their children. He sent love in a form we could comprehend.

We humans do understand law and judgment. We are well-versed in them. But what about love without judgment? What if the Father's love was already as great toward us as we believe it is now since Jesus appeased his wrath? Did God not say, "If you've seen Jesus, you've seen the Father?" What if we believed God's love was an analogy for an earthly parent's love? As a parent, when you held your child the first time, did not your heart swell with a fierce, protective love you'd die to protect? There is seldom a love so fierce as a mother's.

I understand, some parents are so filled with pain due to the way they were raised, they are unable to nurture their child. This isn't normal. It may happen often, and it's heartbreaking, but it's not normal. Many parents, when met with the Father's healing love, receive their first taste of an emotion that speaks of peace they've never known— their hearts melting, liquid love dripping down around their hearts, long held icy for self-preservation.

What if there's no us versus them? What if the truth is, we're out of many, one? What if there are no sides? How great a love has He provided for us to partake in? Perhaps this love, when recognized, will heal the earth and its inhabitants.

CHAPTER 28

heal thyself

Just a few weeks before my twelfth birthday, my mom told me I'd soon have what's known as a period—part of becoming a woman. I heard what she said, but I couldn't wait to scurry away. I wanted nothing to do with that awkward subject. While I loved being a girl, I wanted nothing to do with what becoming a woman meant.

Sure enough, one morning soon after my twelfth birthday, feeling something was different, I rushed to the bathroom to find the tell-tale sign that womanhood had arrived. I got what I needed, sad I'd never be the same, wiped away my tears, and hurried downstairs to help with the daily chores on the farm. I spoke of it to no one.

Fast-forward almost thirty years later, I find myself in a dramatically different state of mind. I've spent more than twenty years studying health and am amazed by the information available to us, yet until recently, we've been so far removed from the home remedies our grandmothers and great-grandmothers used. It's by far most popular to do what our doctor tells us and take prescribed medication than to be taught to know our bodies and listen to the intuition God gifted us with.

I've been through emotional turmoil and used food to cope with the impact of sexual abuse that took place as a child, that part I understand. What I find interesting is, I was so averse to the functions of the female body, I thought my body had betrayed me when I became a woman. But I believe, just as I found peace in my soul, there's also a way of living in which peace leads to wholeness and my body responds by aligning itself to the way it was intended by its Creator.

It became popular during World War II for moms to give their babies formula because moms had to work in factories and fulfill other jobs away from home while the men fought at war. Formula allowed others to take care of the little ones. What was a necessity in those days became the new normal. I remember my mom telling me of choosing to breastfeed as a new mom. Her decision was met with disdain by other mothers who believed using formula was the proper path.

This is just one example of how far removed we have become from how we were designed to live. Isn't it amazing that despite the embrace of breastfeeding in recent years, not so long ago, formula was looked at as better than mother's milk?

I've come to understand the disconnect I felt toward my body and the state of my health in recent years. It really isn't surprising I had the issues I did. I'd seen womanhood as a curse and the functions my body went through each month as something I wished to escape from. I accepted condemnation for the way I thought and lived. I accepted that I deserve to live in poor health and that I didn't deserve better.

If we were designed to feed our bodies with the food God created from the beginning, isn't it little wonder that when we put all kinds of artificial products in our bodies that the body might protest? Hippocrates said, "Let food be thy medicine, and medicine be thy food," but this is much different than what most of us live by today. Hippocrates, who lived in 460 BC, knew the wisdom of putting good food in his body. The main issue they struggled with back in the day was to have clean water and good hygiene. Today, we have access to clean water and good hygiene, but we eat a lot of ingredients the body doesn't recognize as food.

How different might our lives be if we began to seek out the wisdom of the foods our great grandmothers relied on to create balance in the body, such as fermented foods and drinks, herbal teas, garlic, and onions, to name a few. If your great grandmother is still living, why don't you ask her about the foods of her childhood? We pay huge amounts of money for scientists to find cures for many of the diseases prevalent today, but we may be surprised by the wisdom to be found, were we to search for it.

I'm grateful for doctors and the amazing things they're capable of. The feats they've achieved are nothing short of incredible. I look to doctors to bandage me up when cut badly, or set my bone when I break it, but I can't look to them for my health. God created my body to be healthy. It's only when my body and mind are out of balance that disease can manifest. I find balance by eliminating the substances my body dislikes and allowing it to return to a place of rest when I give it foods that bring life.

It's been a long journey from knowing nothing about my body's functions and feeling betrayed by it, to being in awe of its capabilities. I listen to what my body prefers, and it continues to return to a state of balance. I am still imperfect in my journey, but I know balance is available for me. I seek to lean into a physically peaceful way of being in my body, just as I'm at peace with my soul.

I've tried many different diets and was at times a yo-yo dieter. A few years ago, seeking peace with the emotional issues that kept me in an arrested place of development, I purposed to listen to my body. Exhausted by all the research and all the different diets, I've increasingly found peace in the decision to find what my body prefers by listening to it.

This journey included finding peace with the sexual abuse and peace with my body, right where it is, loving it just as it is. Going from despising myself to loving myself has been a challenging journey, to say the least. The outcome is a gift I'm profoundly grateful for. There were many moments along the way I've been tempted to jump on yet another diet plan, but by resisting that urge and seeking each time to get quiet and listen for what my body wants, I've found a greater measure of peace with the struggle that haunted me from the age of twelve.

One of the most challenging issues for women is the ability to love ourselves and embrace these strong, resilient bodies God created us to live in. What if we begin to love ourselves right where we are? What if by looking to the way He designed us and loves us, we find peace for the painful experiences, rest for our weary, battle-worn souls and a victorious life. What if we were able to love ourselves and others fully?

Each challenge we face is an invitation to see differently and learn a new way of being. God being in you, means there's no situation you find yourself in where He's not there.

What if you were to trust His wisdom within to heal your body and direct your path? Often, as with the health of our soul, we listen to the voices of others. We also listen to the many new voices concerning the state and size of our bodies, finding temporary relief and results. Yet when we return to our old habits, our temporary success wanes and all but disappears, gradually returning to its old way of being. What if we embraced a new way?

What if we had peace concerning the state of our bodies and believed God wants us to live in health just as our soul does? What if we knew perfection isn't required? Might we be led to replace the belief that we deserve disease because we make unhealthy choices, with peace in health, which is ours by birthright, regardless our choices? When we believe we deserve bad, we receive bad, even when we don't want it. What if, believing our Creator desires every good thing for us, also leads us to a peaceful way of being in our bodies?

CHAPTER 29

hero worship

One of the most challenging areas in my life has been the fear of not being enough, not as much as someone else—putting little value in myself and my impact on others.

From a young age, I'd point out my flaws to my friends. I wanted to beat them to the punch. I wanted them to know I'm fat and awkward before they had the chance to think it themselves, and I was confident they'd agree with my view of myself.

I longed to be important to others. I wanted above all else to be loved for who I was. I often thought others were so much better at being themselves than I was at being me. I'd look at someone I deemed perfect and wish I could be like them.

After leaving me out of a get-together, there were times friends would later apologize for their treatment of me, confessing jealousy was their reason for leaving me out of the loop. It was never difficult for me to forgive a friend's mistreatment of me, but I could never understand why someone would be jealous of me. I guess it goes to show, we all judge ourselves differently than others do. Just as I thought others had all their ducks in a row, they felt the same about me.

I think this is the very reason we think celebrities, famous authors, a well-known minister, or even the president are the pinnacle of success. We look at their platform and view what they project as importance; that's how we measure success.

The truth is, most of the time, we get to see only what others allow us to see. We don't see the dark moments those we deem important face when in private. The same is true with social media; we see pictures most often shared with the right pose and filter. We appreciate when someone allows us a glimpse into how things really are because we like being reminded everyone else puts their shoes on one at a time, too.

If we could see that each one of us has insecurities about our way of being at one time or another, we'd be more comfortable in our own skin. We'd spend less time trying to explain ourselves or making excuses for our appearance or the state of our house when an unexpected visitor arrives. We wouldn't be so concerned with putting out fires of judgment.

Being ashamed of the girl in the mirror for the way she does life, causes us to want to hide our true selves from others, afraid they'll see the desperation we feel to fit in and be enough. When we realize everyone else is just like us, we begin to be our own kind of beautiful. We don't waste time going after others, seeking to make them shine less bright; instead, we are quick to give each other compliments, supporting each other, remembering we're in this life together.

How much more will we accomplish in life living authentically ourselves, instead of seeking to fit into a mold we think is appropriate? Hero worship is for those who don't know themselves. While meeting an important person by the world's standards may be interesting, when we know ourselves, we'll enjoy learning about that person instead of being excited at the mere fact of meeting a celebrity. We will have conversation in which we will potentially learn something from each other instead of being tongue-tied because we think the important person has something we can only hope to attain.

How much time is wasted seeking to fit in with the crowd? Aren't all of us inspired with authenticity when we see it in another? We tend to think every other person has their stuff together better than we do. What if we could see to a greater degree how loved we are, how complete we are? What would we accomplish by being truly ourselves?

What if there's a touch of heaven on the everyday things, as I once heard a minister say? What if the things that matter most throughout our whole lives are the little things we do each day? We need to love with our whole heart, right where we are, God in us—loving others to wholeness, not demanding they be how we want them to be. Instead, give them permission to find God in their own way, allowing Him to reveal His character to them in a way they understand. In the same way, we should give ourselves permission to not have it all together, giving ourselves the same permission to understand as we're able.

My experience with God is a personal journey of being surprised at every turn that He isn't as I once thought. I expected the journey to look like the teachings of my youth, but it has proven different at each bend in the road. For all the times I was angry with God for dropping the ball, I was delighted many times to know that He was with me all along. He gave me the time to come to a gentle realization that He is who He is regardless of my way of seeing Him. When I quiet my heart and open my mind, He reveals His way of being within me, a beautiful gift. I gain new understanding, being able to participate with Him and what He desires to accomplish on this earth, instead of dragging my feet and demanding things of Him.

If I but listen with an open heart, my journey will be one of new discoveries, being continually surprised by how God's presence manifests in my life. I know the things He's promised, He'll bring to fruition.

When we live in a state of trusting God to show us His precepts, we'll spend less time defending our beliefs and arguing with others to defend our stance, knowing He doesn't need us to defend Him or ourselves. He's weathered many misrepresentations of who He is and is still the same, despite the contrary voices.

Give yourself permission to be your own hero and a hero for others by being authentically you, and in turn, you'll inspire others to discover that being authentically themselves is the best way to be.

CHAPTER 30

a purpose so grand

Throughout the raising of my children, while I loved every sad, happy, frustrating, joy-filled moment, I always struggled with feeling as though I wasn't doing enough. As I fumbled my way through the messy responsibility that is the parenting I loved, I still withheld part of my heart, part of my love. This part of me was occupied with keeping the walls in place. I believed I needed those barriers to survive. Maybe I did need them for a season, but with the walls in place, those closest to me received love from a broken woman, daughter, sister, wife and mother.

I constantly sought to be more, be better, be enough. I was never enough in my own eyes. Every area I'd been broken in tainted everything my hands touched. Through it all, upon reflection, I came to see the ways God touched my life and I knew His hand was on my heart. He gave me quiet support, willing to be what I needed until I came up for air, willing to allow the walls so carefully constructed to crumble piece by piece.

Why is it so often we only see the beauty of our journey upon reflection? What if we could see heaven in our everyday lives? What if we could realize the most important time is right here, right now? That the children who call us mommy or the job we have that requires our skills, the mission field we serve, or the elderly we care for is the most important thing to do right now, and that it's enough?

What if the very places we are broken in because we believe God has betrayed His promises to us are the areas in which He's inviting us to see things differently? Can we find the grace to see things differently than we've always thought?

For the woman who desperately wants to conceive a child and has exhausted every avenue—may you find God in this place of despair. When there are so many who effortlessly conceive and even discard their little one, why can the one who wants a child more than life itself not have a little one to call "my child"? May He reveal his heart to you in a way you can understand, so that the place you're in at this very moment become an invitation to understand something that brings life to you. May your pain be replaced with love, giving you a heart to love others to wholeness. Invite Him to be within you as the only One you need to be whole.

For the woman whose child or spouse has been overtaken by the grip of substance abuse—as you've cried out to God in desperation for the life of your beloved, may you know, there's no need to take responsibility for their choices. As much as you want to fix it, know that the best course of action for you is to find rest with what is. May you find who God wants to be for you in this season, and that you'll be uniquely qualified to give support to another who's experiencing the same.

For the one who's lost a loved one much too soon, I can't begin to comprehend and won't try to give advice. I simply pray that in the greatest space of emptiness, you find the healer of all hearts to be who you need. In knowing the inexpressible loss you didn't ask for and having to exude a strength you don't feel, you can continue, one foot in front of the other. May you know that those who don't know the shoes you wear seek to love and comfort you with the love they know. May you know love that is yet undiscovered.

For the mom who knows the intense pain of a teenager who, just a short while ago, loved you effortlessly, but suddenly lashes out at you as they seek to find their path to adulthood—as my husband reminded me over and over through this process, "Remember you're the adult." While I found his advice frustrating and unwanted at times, it was sound advice. This season isn't for you to react to protect your heart from your teenager's pain. It's a time of allowing them to grow and become ready to do life as an adult, independent of you.

My mom has been my inspiration for this era of parenting. Throughout my teen years, I struggled to get along with my mom. While there were circumstances beyond both our control that caused much of our discord, she walked with a strength I continue to marvel at today. I thought many times she didn't notice my frustration, but I realize today, she chose to be the adult, allowing me to grow into a woman. One of the best gifts I received from my mom was that she parented like the mother eagle, who prepares her young to leave the nest by being as a mother should be, enabling them in the way she conducts her life to grow wings to fly.

Giving your child wings to fly means allowing them to figure life out for themselves as you love, support, and guide them to the best of your ability. One thing I've found is, the more I rest in God's peace and love, the more I'm able to love my children, palms open, trusting them in the journey through bumps, bruises, and all. He is after all, their Father first, just as He is mine.

For the woman who is still broken by a dysfunctional childhood or abuse, may you find peace for your pain and love for the bitterness you developed to survive. May God be to you the love of a Mother you never received or the love of a Father you missed out on, and may you, having known the deepest, loneliest, darkest moments in life, be the one to bring the love you now know through the Father's heart, to the ones who wear the same shoes you do.

My sisters, my keepers: I invite you to walk alongside me, as we bind up the broken, give strength to those too weary to journey on, and heal the gaping wound our mistaken identity has caused us, knowing we're out of many, one—every tribe, every nation, every color. Together, we're stronger, and together, we heal fractured sisterhood, one woman at a time. Together, we find there is no ceiling, for our identity tells the story of warriors, too long having believed we're less than.

CHAPTER 31

through different glasses

Accepting that life is different than the carefully planned future we wanted can create the greatest wrestling within the human heart— the kind of wrestling that leaves us limping due to the imprint it has left.

As a young girl of sixteen, being assured of my religion, and viewing myself as having my ducks lined up in a neat row, I recall stating to my co-worker one day that there had to be something wrong with the wife whose husband wasn't faithful to her.

It was only a few years later when my marriage was on the rocks that the words I'd spoken replayed in my thoughts. I was devastated by the sheer arrogance I'd had, to think I knew anything about this hurting couple and thought myself an authority on relationships. This was only one of many opinions I'd had from youth, where future humble pie was served.

At one of the darkest seasons of my life during the separation between my husband and me, I thought of all the things I was sure of and realized my opinions were unfounded ideas based on my ideology. The heart isn't challenged by looking at a situation from the outside in, but when immersed in the depths of despair. In that place, everything you thought you knew quickly disappears along with judgment of others.

I've no doubt others could have shed light on the struggles I was having, but there are paths we walk as an individual where others may as well be speaking a different language. The heart is often processed by a season of darkness, where you lack direction, but you simply put one foot in front of the other, allowing the long-held ideals and beliefs to be stripped away.

After experiencing a failed marriage that was only by God's grace restored, I came away with love for others concerning their relationships. I was much slower to give my opinion. I realized even when I may see a simple solution for a relationship, there are paths for others to walk through just as I did. Telling another how to walk isn't nearly as effective as their feet walking the path themselves. The understanding we receive through lenses changed by personal experience, works in our hearts a compassion not wrought any other way.

My adult life has been a journey of peeling away layer after layer of ideals instilled by man's idea of how God is and operates, a formula set up to explain God and who He is. While the views I was taught proved effective according to outward appearances, the law skewered my heart and left it broken. Only by allowing the lens I looked through to be challenged, being willing to hear directly from the Father's heart, was I able to weed through all the varying beliefs and come away more compassionate and filled with peace and rest.

Professing Christians are at times the harshest, most critical and judgmental people on earth, I having been one of them. We seem to think we must judge others lest God or other Christians think we're condoning sin. Why was Jesus called a winebibber? Wouldn't it suggest that instead of calling out people for their wrongful acts, He instead loved them? Wasn't it so, each time someone was in His presence, they left a changed person?

My personal experience is, when I appeared to be a model Christian, I was praised for being as I was, a great example of godliness. Yet later, when I outwardly did things deemed unrighteous, the very people who sang my praises were the first to find fault. I hold no ill-will toward anyone. My point is simply this: when we rely on the outward appearances, we can't know when a person is alright. It's only when we look at a person's heart that we're able to see who they really are.

When we remind others who they are in God's eyes, we convict them of their righteousness instead of convicting them of their wrong-doing. Each person knows they make bad decisions at times and fail at right-doing and right-being, but when we remind them who they are and whose they are, we inspire them to live victoriously.

Most often, we require others to live rightly before they can be a part of our lives. We claim to be the salt of the earth, yet we separate ourselves from others, afraid we'll fall away, too. There are many different opinions on Bible verses and I've no doubt most theologians would pounce on these words and tell me just how wrong this is, yet, I ask, what does judgment achieve? It causes those who aren't living by our standards to be driven to the outer courts. Who will love them and bring them in if we require them be clean first?

We're quick to quote, *"Greater is he that is in us than he that is in the world,"*[1] yet we live in fear of he "who is in the world". What if we'd trust the Father's heart within us to keep us? What if we'd give Him free reign to captivate our hearts and teach us His precepts? What if we'd begin to speak life over our nation, instead of seeking to bring the last days to fruition by speaking death to our nation? Who of us will make a difference? Who of us will go out among the highways and byways and love the least of these, instead of sitting on our soap boxes making sure all know we're righteous and don't condone sin?

What if we meet the world with compassion, winning hearts with the God they see within us? What if we look through a new lens?

CHAPTER 32

who we need

Throughout my life, God has been who I needed. When I was being raised in religion, He was to me a God of law who demanded I walk according to rules and regulations through a system developed by man. I sought Him and found Him there.

After the doors of the church of my youth closed, for a season, I went through a parched, dry land where I couldn't see or hear Him. But He was who I needed. He waited for me to allow a few layers of my perception of Him to be peeled away, revealing a God of incredible love I had no idea existed.

Year after year, He's lovingly coaxed and invited me to know Him in new ways, each time proving completely different from what I'd expected. The more layers of deeply ingrained beliefs peeled away, the more my heart gravitated toward Him. His all-encompassing love wooed me to count the cost and follow Him to each new place, even when it threatened my long-held perspective of Him.

If not for all the varying systems of beliefs, who would He be to you? If you stripped away the things you were taught, who would He be to you? Would He be one who surprised you, leaving you in awe of how approachable He is, because He's your Father and will go to the ends of the earth to assure you of His Love? Is He one you have no need to be afraid of? Is He one who invites you to know what He's about? He does want you to participate in bringing heaven to earth.

What if it is man who demands that our life look like the words painted in black and red, according to our interpretation? Has man turned his experience into a system of beliefs with a title, thereby causing us to miss out on God's best? What if God invites us to know Him outside of the book? Yet when we read the book, it bears witness to His Spirit within.

We had just gotten married and were getting settled into our new home when we sat down for dinner. My husband said, "I don't pray before I eat." I was shocked and horrified. I exclaimed, "But what are we going to teach our children?" My husband replied in just a few words, "I don't want to do something just because I was taught I'm supposed to do it. To say my husband's announcement put me in an uncomfortable place was an understatement.

I chewed on it throughout dinner, wondering just who this man was I agreed to spend my life with. Over the next few days, as I contemplated this conversation, I thought back over my life and recalled how my family prayed before and after our meals. I thought about how the moments of silence were called, "putting our hands down." It would make much more sense to say it in German, but in any language, to my young mind, putting my hands down meant being quiet for a few moments. I never stopped and thanked God for our food; instead, my mind wandered from one thought to the next while I waited until someone cleared their throat, signaling we were done putting our hands down and could proceed to fill our growling bellies.

(Author's note: Since writing of this experience, in conversation with my mom, she told of how as a child, her dad asked each one of the children to pray for their meal. There being fourteen of them meant it took a little while. Mom recalled how as they got older, they practiced saying the little prayer as fast as possible. I had always thought that since my dad listened to our prayers at bedtime, that it was his idea for us to say our prayers. I understand today that with many little ones, it proved impossible for my mom to continue listening to our prayers as she would've had there been just a few of us. This by no means takes away from the many hours my dad dedicated to listening to the sweet ramblings of us children as we thought of yet another thing to mention to God during our bedtime routine. I appreciate his love and dedication immensely. This does however, highlight that it's easy for us to remember childhood experiences differently than they were. Although we quit after a time, maybe due to moving to a new Amish community, I had forgotten that I used to say a little prayer before mealtime as a little girl.)

To know my husband is to know a generous man who's quick to express gratitude for the love of His Savior and what God has gifted him with. He doesn't hold to the habits many of us grew up doing just because that's how things are done.

This is just one example of how habits, once part of my belief system, were challenged. It forced me to ask myself why I do what I do. I'm grateful daily for the love and life I've been given and express that gratitude to my Father. There are times when I simply breathe, "Thank you for this amazing food." There are also times when I ask God to bless the food because I'm a little bit scared of the contents of dinner and the impact it might have on my stomach. But it's an expression of gratitude I genuinely feel as opposed to being silent for a few moments or saying a prayer because I'd feel condemned not to.

This life we get to live is a relationship between a Father and His children. By allowing our beliefs to be challenged, while initially scary, we're able to connect with His heart and feel His heartbeat, where He becomes the air we breathe. He loves us with a love that's difficult to describe. He allows us to be how we need to be until we find the grace to change.

There are many different religions in this world, most of which rely on traditions and systems set up by man. Many of us spend most or all our lives living within the confines of the church we belong to, feeling safe within the spiritual walls that were built for us. What if there's a relationship available with the Father in which you don't need pre-set laws to know Him or live a victorious life? What if your heart, upon knowing Him, were to be so captivated by His light that you would want to live right and do good, not because you must to be righteous, but because you know He has made you righteous. When you know your identity is in Him, the fruit of knowing Him includes your heart of worship towards Him and the good fruit that follows.

If God sees Jesus when He looks at us, why do we continue to claim to be a poor beggar who'll be happy just to get into a little corner of heaven? Do we not know we are His sons and daughters, and our inheritance includes ruling and reigning with Him, bringing heaven to earth? Many of us say we are washed in the blood and Jesus is our brother. How then do we claim to be a filthy sinner saved by grace, but still a desperate sinner? Is it not saying what Jesus did was not enough to redeem us? What would happen if we identify with Him, agreeing with how He sees us? Would we not be transformed? Would we not begin to live victorious lives with the love we experience splashing over on all we encounter?

If His Spirit is within us, teaching us all things, is He not then enough to keep us from going astray? Do we still think we need set laws to keep us in line? If we do, are we not saying His redemptive power is not enough? Must we put walls around ourselves because we'll go wrong? What if we simply trust Him to be who we need?

CHAPTER 33

does she love jesus?

The other day, I received a text from one of my cousins telling me she saw a woman at a funeral who looked quite familiar to her. Upon asking, she found the woman was a friend of mine who'd traveled a great distance to attend my wedding more than twenty years ago. We'd only known each other briefly but had become good friends. However, other than writing letters for a few years, as often happens, we'd taken different paths and drifted apart. I haven't seen or heard from her in twenty years. I thought of her often and hoped she was well. My cousin relayed to me that my friend asked only one question about me, "Does she love Jesus?"

It was sweet of my friend from days gone by to ask, and obviously she believed that if the answer to her question was yes, then everything was good. Do you know what would've meant even more? If she had asked, "Does she know that Jesus loves her?"

Most Christians measure everyone by their love for God. I spent my youth trying to love God with all my heart. It was a tormented season in my life as I sought to love God yet found myself falling short with each challenge I faced. It wasn't until I realized God loved me that my life changed. Up to that point, I lived a life of attempting to sacrifice daily to win God's approval and hoping my good deeds and actions would appease Him.

When I experienced His love that bathed my heart in warm liquid oil that flowed into the broken crevices, my life changed. That is when I began to realize it's not about our ability to love Him, it's about His ability to love us. His unconditional and healing love is what changes our hearts and evokes in us a heart that loves him.

We read in the Bible how Peter insisted he loved Jesus, yet he denied knowing Him when challenged in the middle of a large audience. His strength wasn't in how mightily he loved Jesus, for when the chips were down, he denied knowing Him. I have no doubt Peter felt terrible when he walked away after seeing the pain in Jesus' eyes.

In today's world, there are few who truly know Jesus loves them. The church of my childhood focused on living right by our outward actions, and the church of my teen years focused on presenting ourselves a living sacrifice, holy and acceptable unto God. Both are good in part, but without knowing the Father's heart toward us, we focus on what we can do for Him instead of what He's done for us.

He loves us with so great a love; He submitted a part of Himself, in the form of His Son, to die a brutal death to convey the depths of His love for us. Most people in today's world have heard something about God, but few of those want to know God because of the picture we've painted of Him. For too long, we've painted a picture of a

God who demands people walk according to our interpretation of the Bible. We cast aside anyone we believe is living wrong, requesting they first clean up their lives before we share a meal with them. Or, if they leave our circle, we talk about how they've fallen away and there must be something wrong with them; therefore, we no longer associate with them.

Jesus sat with people and ate with them. Each time, His presence left people changed for having met Him. What if we'd live this way? What if people knew God loved them by being with the God within us? What if we loved and shared our time with those who are hurting instead of sitting in our pew, ready to criticize those we're uncomfortable with?

When we focus on God's love for us, our hearts overflow with gratitude. When we see His goodness toward us, we love to please Him, but our standing with Him isn't in how successful we are in walking rightly. Our standing with Him is determined by His love for us; when He looks at us, He sees Jesus. When we agree with His view of us, we live victoriously, not without faults and failures but a life of seeing His goodness, our lives reflecting Him.

I sought for years to love Him. I sought to know Him. I found it was a difficult journey from law to grace. I've frequently heard the term "greasy grace" from those who prefer the law. I know people are concerned with those who take grace as a license to sin, yet, does someone who uses grace as license to sin really understand what grace is? For me, grace has proved to be everything that encompasses Jesus, and in His reflection, my heart is compelled to love and live in what makes His heart glad. From that place, my heart swells with the love I receive from my Creator and returns goodness to Him and to those I encounter daily.

Grace is God's perfect love toward us. Grace is knowing His love, his heart, and everything He is. Grace is seeing we are completely loved and accepted by our Father. Grace begets love, right living, and gratitude. Looking upon grace evokes in God's children a desire to return the love they receive from their Father. They have no desire to do that which saddens their Father's heart.

If someone asked my son if he loves his mom, and if that were their only concern, wouldn't that sound a bit weird? Wouldn't you expect someone to ask my son how he is and how his mom is doing? Along the same line of thought, would I daily ask him to prove his love for me by doing set actions? Would I delight in his daily efforts to appease my wrath so I might accept him, or, would I, as his mom, be happy when he goes about his life, building dreams and being successful in what he creates, confident in my love for him?

Having childlike faith is taking God's love for me for granted. It is full confidence that He is my Daddy, his heart toward me is good, and there's nothing I can do to change His heart toward me. I might make him sad, but He doesn't love me any less. While some would say we owe Him a debt of gratitude, I ask you, do you require your children to thank you every day for what you've given them? Do you want them to beg you to forgive them daily for their mistakes? Or, does it make your heart glad when they walk confident in your love for them, randomly expressing gratitude because they appreciate your love and all the things you've done for them?

It makes my heart glad when you know Jesus loves you.

CHAPTER 34

agree with me

Have you ever noticed when you do or buy something new, you notice that new thing everywhere you look? For instance, when you have your house painted, you'll notice all the houses that need to be painted or the ones that look as crisp and clean as yours. This often proves the same with things we believe.

Lauren, a beautiful, talented woman who had a great education was hired by a company that provided a great income for her. By all appearances, she had a life many envied, yet if you got to know her, you'd find she struggled intensely with the need for others to agree with her opinions of things.

Lauren had many friends. When she was having a difficult time with someone, she'd call her friend Tammy. If Tammy didn't give Lauren the answers she wanted to hear, she'd call her friend Jan to vaguely hint that Tammy seemed to have a bit of a problem, but never outright say something definitive. If Jan picked up on the clue, asking about the problem, Tammy would become the subject of the conversation to manipulate Jan into agreeing with Lauren about her side of the story. Before Jan knew what had happened, she had bought into Lauren's story that not only was her view on the issue right, but Tammy wasn't a good friend who'd stick by her.

Little by little, Lauren's circle of friends shrunk. Over time, each friend heard from another and realized Lauren manipulated each of them at some point to get the outcome she desired. Lauren felt hurt and thought it was impossible to have good friends. With no friends left, Lauren began to reflect on her habits.

While at the airport one day, Lauren was waiting to board a flight home from a business trip when she overheard a conversation between two strangers. "You can always go far enough to find someone to agree with you," said the lady next to her, "It's when someone challenges your beliefs that it counts." Lauren realized she was controlling her friendships by requiring others to agree with her. Upon reflection, she became aware she had exhausted herself to stay in good standing with everyone, but she had driven her friends away instead.

The flip side of Lauren's experience is when we know we're wrong and still take time to listen, we'll find there are always important new perspectives for us to see. When we allow our beliefs to be challenged, we'll find either the beliefs hold, or they change, and we'll be better off for it with our friends benefitting in the process as well.

Many times, we continue childhood habits into adulthood which are not healthy. When we allow differences in opinion and beliefs to open our hearts and minds, we'll find the courage to admit it may be time to change our habits. When we no longer feel the need to hide behind a perfect façade, we can show who we truly are and find our friends love and appreciate seeing the real us; in turn, they'll be inspired to be real also.

Without the need to fit in, the term, "keeping up with the Joneses" wouldn't exist. How much would our world shift if we would embrace ourselves as we are, freely living who we are?

From a young age, we learn to know what it feels like to have others make fun of us for how we are. Some of us, attempting to fit in, change how we are, while others let it flow off their backs. A prime example happened when I was a little girl. One of the boys at school made fun of me for the way I ran. I made a conscious effort to change the way I ran. That resolution followed me into adulthood.

My daughter, on the other hand, had a classmate from school tell her, "You're weird!" My daughter's response was, "Thanks!" And that was the end of it for her. She let it roll off her back and never gave it another thought. I heard this transpire, and it was one of those teaching moments you only experience by observing. My daughter inspired me, the adult. I purposed to be more authentic. So what, if someone thinks I run weird?

How different would our children's lives be if we would simply remind them it's fine to be different? I recently read a book by a lovely young woman who lives in Uganda. She adopted a number of girls who had no family. While an inspiring story, one of the details that really stood out to me was when she related how other children made fun of her adopted daughters for having a white mother. The mom's response assured her daughters that the other children only made fun of them because they were different. This highlighted for me much of what I already believed to be true. In a country where the poverty is greater than most of us can imagine, even there, children make fun of those who are different. It's all in how we respond to our children when someone says something hurtful.

I have a cousin who I admire. Upon her child's complaint that another child called him stupid, she asked, "Well, is it true? Are you stupid?" He replied, "No." She encouraged him to go out and play. Had my cousin cried with her son, as she may have felt like doing, his memory of that day would be entirely different. He may have lost confidence in who he was if his mom apologized for the other child's rudeness and made a big fuss over the incident.

Much of what we learn in life comes from the example of those who train us. Even we adults are often prejudiced when others are different or do things differently. We like to be comfortable in our well-structured boxes and feel threatened by those who are different.

What would our world look like if we were to lay down our ideals, prejudices, and demands to keep things as they are? Instead, we could embrace differences, seek to understand each other and remember we are out of many, one.

When we know who we are, it doesn't matter what anyone says about us—we know they are simply ignorant. We don't have to carry what misinformed people think of us. We get to be the bigger person, showing what it means to disable the bully and what confidence should look like.

There are many children who don't have a positive influence in their lives to remind them they're loved and valued. May we take each chance we get to be that positive influence and change the course of those children's lives. When we touch one child with love, we impact them, their future spouse, their children, grandchildren, and generations to come, creating an environment that remembers we're all different, yet the same. This allows us to stand where we are without the need for others to agree with us.

CHAPTER 35

the words you speak

"…life and death are in the power of the tongue…"[1]

This verse has a way of highlighting truth in many different situations, but one of the most impacting times was after the release of my first book. Upon hearing some feedback of my story, which I admit was secondhand; the effect was what it was intended to be. I was devastated by the comments because of who they came from. Picking my heart up off the floor, I reminded myself that the comments originated from a heart that loves, so I must choose to receive the opinion constructively.

As I wrestled with it over the next few days, I would go from wanting to yell at the person for not understanding the pain and process I walked through to get the long-hidden words on paper. They did not know to appreciate the courage it took to give those words to the world to do with as they choose. They did not know releasing those words and experiences allowed my heart to return to peace.

What it taught me, as many painful experiences do, was to remind me of the many times I'd callously commented on something I had read. There were good parts to a certain book, but I certainly didn't agree with that author on some of their points of view. I never realized the effect my words would have had on the author, had they received my feedback. That's the beauty of painful lessons. They hurt, but they teach, and they leave us changed with a little more compassion.

These lessons are, after all, the best way for us to learn the power of our words. Today, I'm slower to volunteer my opinion about other people's actions and deeds. I realize I'll never know the innermost turmoil and challenges they faced throughout their journey. The motivation for their words and actions belongs to them alone.

The important thing to remember is the fact I had heard the comments second-hand. If I've learned one thing about second-hand comments, it's this: each person hears things according to their perception, impacting the delivery of words. The person who replayed the initial comments wanted me to know they supported me regardless what others think. For all I know, the person changed a few key words to make themselves the hero for me. The beautiful gift is, I may never know, and that's alright. The intended purpose was to teach me the power of my words, and it accomplished that. I'm grateful.

This experience also worked on my life-long need to be accepted. I often choose the safest path so others don't have a problem with me, keeping my head down and going quietly with the flow. This worked for a season, but we can flow along with the crowd for just so long before we must give our beliefs air to breathe, and share the things hidden away lest we die with the words still buried.

Increasingly, my need to be accepted has waned as I have grown in the knowledge of who I am to God. I'm His beloved and He accepts me unconditionally. His love gives me courage to grow bolder in my beliefs. I am no longer obsessed with others' approval of me. I choose to let the world do with the beliefs as they will.

I've heard often how people will judge you regardless how you live, making your journey towards self-acceptance necessary. I understand that to a greater degree than ever before. We spend much of our lives seeking to fit in and not cause any ripples because we desperately want to win others' approval. We choose to be a copycat instead of living authentically. While being authentic is challenging, it's the freest way to live, and I'm frequently reminded that if I'm not me, who will be? If I don't write my story, who will?

I heard a minister tell how his father shared with him that there are boxes and boxes on the shelves of heaven. These boxes of all shapes and sizes remain unopened. Many people never opened their gifts of talents, because they wanted to fit in with the status quo. When the people die, these boxes remain unopened forever. I'm sure this is just an analogy, but it inspired me to use the gifts and talents I've been given to leave my unique imprint on this world.

Each one of us has a unique way of experiencing life and seeing things. If we choose to be authentic ourselves, we have something to share with others that has never been given before with our unique flavor. Why would we seek to fit in? May we remind ourselves and those we love to be who God created them to be—a person who loves others and with that love, brings healing to those they meet throughout the course of their lives.

This world has enough judgment to last for all of eternity. What if we decide to feed on His love, reminding each other who we are and whose we are? How much more will others be inspired to know their Father when we show them the love we've known, rather than meeting them with judgment lest our fear of being found in their shoes shows our hidden colors?

The words we speak either give life or death. May we choose life in every area and conversation. May we, when hearing a less than savory comment about someone else, let it die with us, choosing to remind each other to see others as God sees them. With a little more love and less judgment, we'll be reminded we are out of many, one. We'll look at each other and see Jesus instead of the ugliness of judgment when we disagree on points and opinions. We get to choose what proceeds out of our mouths. Let it be love. Let us inspire each other to choose each other. Let peace be the habit of our being.

CHAPTER 36
standard of grace

Within the different religions, there are varying degrees of grace, from intense personal sacrifice required to no sacrifice required. Most of us fall somewhere between these two. Those who require some, say those who require none are supporters of "greasy grace."

Those who require sacrifice, focus on the wrath they believe God feels toward those who don't live according to their religious standards of righteousness. This wrath motivates them to live rightly so they don't get cast into hell.

What if there's a standard of grace so wonderful that it evokes your loyalty with its love? What if He's all love and no wrath? What if you found He wasn't angry at all and loved you with the heart of a Father? You can run as far as you choose, yet He still waits for your heart to receive the love He holds for you. Does He not leave the ninety-nine to seek out the one? If He leaves the ninety-nine to seek out the one, does that not suggest the one is His child, and He is not angry but instead desires the one to be reunited with the ninety-nine, safe in the fold?

How would we respond, were we to realize He loves us and isn't angry? Therefore, we don't have to go to Him just because we want to avoid hell. Instead, we go to Him, because He offers solace for all our pain and suffering the lack of His presence causes us? To me, hell has always been where God was not. For years I sought him, in pain from the religion that withheld His love until I became appropriately righteous. I was unable to attain that standard and begged to see His countenance. When I found the peace He offered, my life was forever changed.

Living by His grace, we get to live in a place of habitation. Gone are the days of needing yet another revival meeting to get our hearts right with God, instead, we get to abide with Him daily. He's already forgiven all. *"This is the work of God, that ye believe on Him whom He hath sent."*[1] *"And He is the propitiation for our sins: and not for ours only, but also for the sins of the whole world."*[2]

We are at peace because we know He works all things together for the good *"to them that love God, to them who are the called according to His purpose."*[3] That means all of us. We who bear the DNA of the One who created us have hearts that seek to return to the love we were born by.

As His children, we get to hear His voice individually. He, our Father, knows us and we, His children, know His voice. Isn't it exciting then to live this life, a journey of discovering the Father's heart? When we think everything is done by reading the words of the Bible with the interpretation of whatever religion we belong to, we settle into trying to live right while waiting for heaven. We tell ourselves that we only need to hold on until we get to heaven when the life we were created for begins.

What if, by His voice within us, we get to discover new things about Him? The purpose of our journey on this earth is to know Him, walk with Him, and partner with Him to bring heaven to earth. How sad it would be to live our lives waiting to get to heaven to know God and our identity in Him, only to die and find heaven actually began here. We have provision to know Him and participate with Him in bringing heaven to a broken and hurting world.

What if, in knowing Him and knowing His immense love, we judge a little less and love a little more—listen a little more and speak a little less? Knowing we needn't decide who's right and who's wrong, we can entrust each one to God, knowing He'll take care of each of the ones He created.

In the forty plus years of my life, if I've learned anything, it's that I've judged often and eventually found myself in a place of uncertainty. Where I'd been so sure of my own opinion on matters, after falling on my face, I came to realize how little I knew after all. I've found it's better to love more and judge less. For how can I know your journey unless I walk a mile in your shoes?

We human beings know about sacrifice. We know about demanding others live by our standard of grace. Do we know, though, about love? Do we know about grace that forgives all, as we've been forgiven all? Even with the darkest places we've visited, dark places that have left us broken, we await a rescuer who will restore us from the devastation. Can we find the grace to look upon those who left us mangled and bruised through the eyes of a Savior who saw their suffering before their suffering turned into our pain?

Can we see them as the once-upon-a-time innocent child who found their world turned upside-down by the ones who should've protected them, thus eliminating the need for our restoration because it would've never happened in the first place? Can we find it in our hearts to restore them by offering forgiveness where judgment is surely deserved?

Each painful situation we find ourselves in earns us the right to be angry and bitter. Instead, what if we choose to love as we've been loved, forgive as we've been forgiven, restore as we've been restored by our Creator? Is it possible to be restored when we tightly hold onto the bitterness that developed after the pain became too much to bear, the day our world as we knew it was shattered? It's by His grace we find the ability to love, forgive, and restore.

If we're going to measure, may we measure by a standard of grace that knows no bounds. If we're going to forgive, may we forgive with the measure with which we have been forgiven. If we're going to love, may we love with the measure we've been loved—an everlasting, restorative, all-encompassing grace.

CHAPTER 37

vulnerability

One of the most challenging areas in my life has proven to be the practice of vulnerability. I find it easy to give gifts and my time, but I find it incredibly challenging to give me. I struggle immensely with intimacy. The culture I grew up in didn't express love with physical touch.

I gave my mom goodnight kisses every night at bedtime, but soon after the age of fourteen, even that stopped. Physical touch wasn't expressed except with my young siblings. It's simply how things were done.

I remember my aunt telling me that my cousin who had a son out of wedlock was instructed to quit being physically expressive with him after he reached aged seven or so, because it would make him *kindisch* (German for childish, silly, underdeveloped or immature).

It's my understanding that most Amish do not believe in physical touch other than a handshake. That was certainly my experience. Once I reached my teen years, I craved physical touch from boys or men intensely, but having been warned never to let a young man know I was attracted to him, I was safe from seeking out physical touch from men. I hid my emotions lest I be dubbed one of those boy-crazy girls.

Today, I find it easy to be expressive with physical touch with my children and my husband. I am growing in this area with the rest of my family also. Little by little, I'm getting used to allowing closeness to those I love most.

I have no doubt sexual molestation from a young age impacted my ability to express physical touch. I couldn't trust anyone to have motives that wouldn't hurt me. Even when I didn't want someone to touch me, I couldn't stand up for myself. I let others cross boundaries I was uncomfortable with, simply pretending nothing was happening until they stopped touching me. Then I would escape to the privacy of my room where I would cry in such pain.

Being vulnerable means to allow others to see the real you. We so often do things to hide our true feelings and emotions. It's the very reason we try to be like everyone else, so others don't see our desperate need to be loved. The beautiful gift of vulnerability is that when we know we're loved, we don't feel the need to hide. We feel increasingly comfortable to let our vulnerability show. We don't feel the need to be who we're not.

After healing the impact of boundaries that were not meant to be crossed, we are able to speak up for ourselves. We give ourselves permission to say what we want and don't want, fully anticipating others will respect our wishes without fear of them no longer liking us.

Many times, we hide from vulnerability, being quick to lash out at others in judgment lest we be found weak and appear less than others. Isn't it true that we always admire those who practice vulnerability? It always encourages us to allow our true colors to show. Each time someone is vulnerable, we're moved by their candidness, helping us to let go just a little bit more of our white-knuckled grip on our emotions.

Most of us spend all our lives letting others see what we feel we control. We base our lives on the impression of others and what's deemed appropriate. For many of us, while we admire others' vulnerability, we try to create the illusion of having all things perfectly in order.

What if we decide to be authentically us, choosing each day to tell those we love how we truly feel about them? What if we no longer hide behind an act? Can we, instead, allow others see the real us, and in turn, give them the freedom to be authentically themselves, too?

One beautiful gift God gave us is the ability to know who we are in Him, becoming bold as we represent our unique voice, story, and life. When we know this, we live true to our story instead of seeking to help others write theirs. We realize that in living true to ourselves, the story that is uniquely ours will be written, and not left as an unopened box returned to God, the packaging tape still undisturbed.

When we're comfortable in our identity, we no longer feel the need to keep up appearances. Instead, we find the courage to show our true colors, knowing we're secure in His approval of us, even if no one else approves.

If we begin to live authentically and by example inspire our children to write their own story, too, there's no bully on earth who can sway them from seeking to live true to who they are. When the bully loses impact, there's no ammunition left to intimidate another.

Soon there will be more people living authentically and fewer individuals left to play copycat. Think about those we admire: it's certainly not the imitators. It's the trailblazers who write as it has never been written before.

Be inspired by the authentically written stories you read and allow them to inspire authenticity in you. Be the one who sets an example for another, so that by your life, they decide to live authentically, too. What if your authenticity inspires others to a greater measure than any other thing you do in this life?

Out of all the millions of people on earth, God decided we needed one of you. No one else is you. No one else can tell your story the way you do, whether you tell it, write it, or love others by it. Living your story is the best gift you can give to others. Allow the painful things you've experienced to teach you the life lessons that enable you to bring healing to others.

It's easy to keep blaming our parents and other guardians of our childhood, but how will that propel us into a victorious life? Will we accomplish a life well-lived when we stay hung up in our bitterness because of our mistreatment, or will we better serve those we meet with love? We must let love not only heal the darkest recesses of our hearts but let that dark place be filled with the light of His love, so that it splashes on those we meet.

Each person on earth loves others to the best of their ability. Many love with lack because they were loved with lack. Sometimes, our greatest gifts come in dark packages. Jesus desires our hearts to be made whole, and in being made whole, we bring healing to others, no matter the depths of darkness we've known in the past.

Being vulnerable means being authentic. May you be the authentic one. May you know the depths of His love for you and just how much He desires for you to live a life of fullness. May you find the courage to live, love, and be with your whole heart. I'm grateful for you, my sister, my friend. Even if we haven't met yet, I'm your fan and wish you the most love.

about the author

Kate Troyer is an author, speaker and advocate for women. Her passion is to help you find your path to heart-healing while embracing your true identity so that you can live and lead from a place of wholeness.

After being raised in an Amish home and transitioning to Mennonite as a teenager, Kate is familiar with the twists and turns life can take without full consent. Having done the work of discovering her own identity outside of those cultures, she values the gift of being able to help others find theirs.

Kate's mission is to walk with those thrust into a shell of shame, religious manipulation, and insignificance, and gently help them shed the layers of other people's opinions of them and live free. Her message will encourage you to confidently embrace who you are so you can lead with authority where you are called.

Kate resides on a small farm in Northeast Ohio along with her husband, two children and an ever-expanding menagerie of animals.

CONNECT WITH KATE

KateTroyer.me
Facebook - @gracefulwarrior.int
IG – Kate.Troyer.Author
Twitter - @KateTroyer1

She Speaks is a powerful story of hope and redemption as Kate Troyer takes you on a journey through her childhood including the pain of believing lies about who she was, anxiety, despair, sexual molestation, and the struggle of being overweight from using food as a way to cope and protect herself from circumstances beyond her control.

Kate shares the darkest moments in her life and the beauty of the broken road that brought her to who she is today, a strong woman of courage and resilience who is grateful for the hard things that created within her a heart of great compassion for others.

The things that were meant to destroy Kate became her gift because once the painful lies she believed were uncovered, they became powerful truths to equip her to live a life of abiding peace and a resounding sense of wholeness.

endnotes

Note: All verses are taken from the King James Version of the Bible unless otherwise noted.

CHAPTER 2

1. Galatians 3:28 (NIV)

CHAPTER 6

1. Mark 12:31
2. Romans 1:16

CHAPTER 7

1. Psalm 139:14
2. Jeremiah 31:3
3. Jeremiah 1:5

CHAPTER 9

1. 1 Timothy 6:4

CHAPTER 19

1. Proverbs 18:21

CHAPTER 21

1. John 2:27

CHAPTER 31

1. 1 John 4:4

CHAPTER 35

1. Proverbs 18:21

CHAPTER 36

1. John 6:29
2. 1 John 2:2
3. Romans 8:28

works cited

The Bible. King James Version. *BibleGateway.com*, https://www.biblegateway.com/versions/King-James-Version-KJV-Bible/. Accessed November 2017.

The Bible. New International Version. *BibleGateway.com*, www.biblegateway.com/versions/New-International-Verison-NIV-Bible/. Accessed November 2017.

www.ingramcontent.com/pod-product-compliance
Lightning Source LLC
Chambersburg PA
CBHW051832090426
42736CB00011B/1771